Contents

Planning Ahead

WHEN TO GO

Barcelona has no off-season—there is always something to see and do. However, May to June and mid-September to mid-October are ideal visiting times, with perfect temperatures and bearable crowds. Summer can be very hot, and you'll have to contend with huge crowds everywhere you go.

TIME

Spain is 6 hours ahead of New York City, 9 hours ahead of Los Angeles, and 1 hour ahead of the UK.

AVERAGE DAILY TEMPERATURES

JAN	FEB	MAR	APR	MAY	JUN	JUL	AUG	SEP	OCT	NOV	DEC
57°F	59°F	63°F	66°F	72°F	77°F	84°F	84°F	81°F	73°F	64°F	59°F
14°C	15°C	17°C	19°C	22°C	25°C	29°C	29°C	27°C	23°C	18°C	15°C

Spring (March to May) is a good time to visit; pleasantly warm, though it can be cloudy.
Summer (June to September) is the hottest season with very high temperatures during July and August.
Autumn (October to November) is normally Barcelona's wettest season, with heavy rain and thunderstorms as summer heat abates.
Winter (December to February) brings rain up to Christmas, followed by cooler, dryer weather, though temperatures are rarely much below 50°F.

WHAT'S ON

January *Three Kings* (6 Jan): The kings arrive by boat and shower children with sweets.
February/March *Carnival*: Boisterous pre-Lenten celebrations include a major costumed procession and the symbolic burial of a sardine. Sitges *Carnival* is particularly colourful.
Easter Celebrated in style in the city districts with a southern Spanish population.
April *St. George's Day* (23 Apr): The festival of Catalonia's patron saint is marked by lovers' gifts: roses for the woman, a book for the man. There are open-air book fairs and impressive floral displays.
June/July *Midsummer* (23–24 Jun): An excuse for mass partying and spectacular firework displays on Montjuïc and Tibidabo. *Festival del Grec* (Jun–Jul): A festival of music, theatre, and dance.
August *Festa Major de Gràcia*: Ten days of street celebrations in the city's most colourful suburb, village-like Gràcia.
September *Diada de Catalunya* (11 Sep): Flags wave on the Catalan National Day, and political demonstrations are likely. *Festa de la Mercé* (24 Sep): The week-long festival honouring the city's patron saint, Our Lady of Mercy, is Barcelona's biggest. Music, theatre, flamenco dancing, parades, fireworks, and spectacles featuring giants, dragons, and *castellers* (human towers) all occur.
December *The Christmas Season*: Preparations include a grand crib in Plaça Saint Jaume (► 43) and a market in front of the cathedral.

BARCELONA ONLINE

www.barcelonaturisme.com
Barcelona's official tourist website has a wealth of information covering every aspect of the city. In English, and regularly updated, it's the obvious place to research your trip. One word of warning—the site can be slow to download.

www.tourspain.es
The main Spanish tourist board site is loaded with detail about both Barcelona and its environs.

www.barcelona-metropolitan.com
The city's premier English language magazine gives the low-down on what's on and what's new in the bar, restaurant, and nightclub scene as well as inspiration for days out of town and a handy classified section for apartments and jobs.

www.hotelconnect.co.uk
A wide range of options in Barcelona—if your first choice is fully booked they'll offer similar accommodation in the same price range

www.bestbarcelonahotels.com
A good choice of mid-range, mid-price hotels with online booking.

www.bcn.es
This site, in English, is run by Barcelona's city council and is primarily aimed at locals. There is an excellent museum section, with up-to-date details of opening times, exhibitions, and more.

www.tmb.net
All you need to know about fares, routes, and the timetables of Barcelona's bus and metro systems.

www.fcbarcelona.com
Even if you're not a football fan, this official site gives an insight to the passions the team evokes.

USEFUL WEBSITES

www.fodors.com
A complete travel-planning site. You can research prices and weather; book air tickets, cars, and rooms; ask questions (and get answers) from fellow travellers; and find links to other sites.

www.renfe.es/ingles
The official site of Spanish National Railways.

www.wunderground.com
Good weather forecasting, updated thrice daily.

CYBERCAFÉS

easyEverything
�� G9 ✉ Ramblas 31
☎ 93 318 24 35 🕐 Daily, 24 hrs 💷 €3 per hour.

Cyberclub
🔂 G9 ✉ C/Sant Pau 124 ☎ 93 442 11 04
🕐 Daily 10–8.30
💷 €1.50 per hour.

El Café del Internet
🔂 P7 ✉ Avda de las Corts Catalanas 656
☎ 93 412 19 15 🕐 Daily 10–midnight 💷 €3/hr.

Cybermundo
🔂 G8 ✉ Bergara 3
☎ 93 317 71 42 🕐 Daily 9AM–1AM 💷 From €1.50 per hour.

Getting There

INSURANCE

US citizens should check their insurance coverage and buy a supplementary policy as needed. EU nationals receive medical treatment with form E111—obtain this form before travelling. Full health and travel insurance is still advised.

MONEY

The euro is the official currency of Spain. Notes in denominations of 5, 10, 20, 50, 100, 200, and 500 euros and coins in denominations of 1, 2, 5, 10, 20, and 50 cents, and 1 and 2 euros were introduced on 1 January 2002.

€10

€50

€200

€500

ARRIVING

Barcelona's modernized airport is at El Prat de Llobregat, 7 miles from the city. Terminal A serves non-Spanish airlines, Terminal B serves Iberia flights. Barcelona is served by 32 international airlines and has direct flights to more than 80 international destinations.

FROM BARCELONA AIRPORT (EL PRAT)

Barcelona's airport (☎ 93 298 38 38) is well served by city links. The convenient Aerobus service connects both terminals with Plaça de Catalunya via Plaça d'Espanya and Gran Via de les Corts (and Sants station for travel to the airport). The service operates every 12 minutes in both directions, from early morning until at least 10PM. The journey takes around 30 minutes and costs €3.15.

Trains link the airport with Sants, Plaça de Catalunya, Arc de Triomf, and Clot-Aragó stations. They run every 30 minutes, from 6.13AM to 11.40PM, and cost around €2.15 one-way. The journey time to Plaça de Catalunya is 25 minutes. Taxis are available outside the airport terminals; the journey takes around 20–30 minutes, depending on traffic, and costs €18–22.

ARRIVING BY TRAIN

Barcelona is connected to all major cities within Spain and a number of destinations in Europe, namely Paris, Geneva, Zürich, and Milan. These trains arrive and depart at Sants Estació, the city's main station, which also has regular bus and metro services to the centre and elsewhere. A few regional trains leave from the stations Estació de França in the old town (predominantly south bound) and Passeig de Gracía in the new town (mainly north bound).

ARRIVING BY BUS
Direct bus services operate from several European countries. The bus station is Estació d'Autobus Barcelona Nord ☎ 902 26 06 06; www.barcelonanord.com.

ARRIVING BY CAR
Barcelona is connected by the AP7 toll *autopista* to the French frontier and motorway network at La Jonquera (90 miles northeast). Toulouse is 245 miles north via N152, the French frontier at Puigcerdà and RN20. Motorway access to the rest of Spain is via *autopista* AP2 and AP7.

ARRIVING BY SEA
Car ferry services from Britain to Spain are operated by Brittany Ferries (☎ 0870 366 53 33, Plymouth–Santander) and by P&O European Ferries (☎ 0870 242 4999, Portsmouth–Bilbao). Ferry services operate to the Balearic Islands from the Port of Barcelona (☎ 93 443 13 00). One of the largest ferry operators is Trasmediterranea (☎ 902 45 46 45).

GETTING AROUND
There are five metro (subway) lines, identified by number and colour. Direction is indicated by the name of the station at the end of the line. The metro runs Mon–Thu 5AM–midnight, Fri, Sat, and the evening before a public holiday 5AM–2AM, and Sun 6AM–midnight.
Buses run 6.30AM–10PM. The free *Guía d'Autobus Urbans de Barcelona* details routes. As well as one-way tickets, several types of *targeta* (travelcard) can be used on the metro and buses.
Barcelona's black-and-yellow taxis can be hailed when displaying a green light and the sign *Lliure/Libre* (free), or can be picked up at a number of taxi ranks. For more information about public transportation ➤ 91.

ENTRY REQUIREMENTS

Anyone entering Spain must have a valid passport (or official identity card for EU nationals). Nationals of Australia and South Africa require a valid passport plus visa.
Visa regulations are subject to change, check the current situation before booking your trip.

VISITORS WITH DISABILITIES

Transport and general access is patchy but improving. For getting around, buses and taxis are the best bet; the *Guia de Autobuses Urbans* shows all wheelchair accessible routes, or call ☎ 93 486 07 52. The Taxi Amic service (☎ 93 420 80 88) has wheelchair adapted taxis; call well in advance to book. Line 2 of the metro has lifts and ramps at all stations. New buildings and museums have excellent facilities for visitors with disabilities, though some older attractions have yet to be converted. For further information, contact Institut Municipal de Disminüits (✉ Avda Diagonal 233 ☎ 93 413 27 75).

Living
Barcelona

Barcelona Now

Above: *the Font Monumental in the Plaça d'Espanya*
Above right: *Festa de la Mercé–Barcelona's biggest festival*

Barcelona, capital of Catalunya, is among Europe's great late 20th-century success stories, a visually stunning, world-class city for all seasons. Europeans flock here for short city-breaks and it is also high on the must-see list for tourists from further afield. Catapulted to international fame by the immense urban renewal project associated with the 1992 Olympics, Barcelona today is an acknowledged leader in cutting-edge style, a let-your-hair-down city that parties against a backdrop of architectural splendour.

It is the architecture that draws many visitors, for no other European city has a greater concentration of art nouveau, know here as *modernisme*.

DISTINCT NEIGHBOURHOODS

• **Barri Gòtic, Cuitat Vella, La Rambla, El Raval, La Ribera** comprise the old city, set back from the waterfront. **L'Eixample** (the Extension) and **Gràcia** are crossed by broad 19th-century avenues and grid-pattern streets. **Port Vell, Barceloneta** and the **Port Olímpic** stretch along the waterfront and beach areas. **Montjüic**, a hill to the southwest, has green spaces and fine museums, while **Tibidabo**, to the north, is residential.

Nineteenth-century industrial prosperity ensured that Barcelona underwent major expansion in the second half of the century, notably in the area of the city called L'Eixample—literally, the Extension. The spacious streets and exotic Modernist buildings here contrast superbly with Barcelona's medieval buildings, concentrated along the narrow streets of the Barri Gòtic, the once-walled old city area. Here, Catalan Gothic churches and palaces are witness to the city's 13th-century wealth and importance, just as *modernisme* structures attest 19th-century industrial power. Against these two marvellously contrasting architectural styles rise the 20th-century's contributions, glitteringly elegant structures of steel and glass, radiating the urban confidence of a city at ease with itself.

Barcelona's modern self-esteem is hardly surprising given the huge social, cultural, and economic changes in the city. Authorities determined to reverse the policies of the previous regime; Catalan was re-introduced as the official language, and the floodgates were opened to a surge of new freedoms and

Above: *café in the high-ceilinged Hivernacle*

STREET ART

• Scattered over the city are more than 100 new squares and parks created during the 1980s to incorporate sculptures by big-name artists, commissioned by the city. Works by Joan Miró, Frank Gehry, Roy Lichtenstein and Claes Oldenberg, to name a few, make Barcelona one of the best cities in the world to view public sculptures.

Above: *Drassanes and Museu Marítim*
Above right: *Museu d'Art Contemporani*

OLYMPIC CITY

• Hosting the 1992 Olympic Games transformed the city in to a thriving metropolis. In 2004 the Universal Forum of Cultures offered world-class performances, theatre, and art exhibitions, and the newly regenerated coastal zone has new bathing areas, a marine zoo, and a promenade that extends 8 kilometres north of the Olympic Village.

energies. The creation of a distinct Catalan style went hand in hand with urban renewal, contributing to a new-style city epitomized by the razzmatazz surrounding the 1992 Olympics. Since then, the pace has continued and the city's reputation as a major player on the world stage is firmly established, standing apart from other Spanish cities and uniquely as itself.

Thriving and confident, and above all, Catalan, Barcelona's main role is that of the capital of Spain's most vibrant autonomous region, contributing a good percentage of Spain's overall industrial output. Hand in hand with this goes its role as one of Europe's most stylish and happening cities, a mix that draws tourists from all over the world. It's an easy place to enjoy; getting around is simple, and the museums splendid, and there's a wide choice of accommodation, restaurants, and bars. The old heart of the city, set around the Rambla, one of the world's most famous streets, is crammed with delights within short walking distance. Further afield from this old core are scattered other attractions and monuments—the great museums, Modernist gems, and other individual

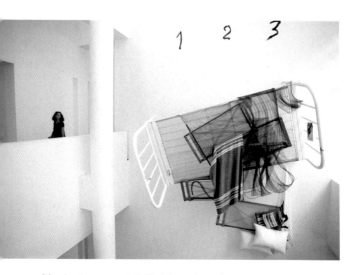

and fascinating areas. Sprinkled throughout the city are wonderfully green spaces, havens of shade and peace during the hot summers. Summer too, is the best time to appreciate Barcelona's re-developed waterfront areas and beaches, an added bonus to any Mediterranean

BARCELONA'S FAMOUS

● Barcelona's civic identity is intrinsically linked to the unique architecture of **Antoni Gaudí** (1852–1926); genius of the *modernista* movement renowned for his organic structures and distinctive pinnacles. His best known work is the Sagrada Familia (➤ 39). While work progressed on this masterpiece, Gaudí was tragically run over by a tram and died unidentified in hospital. When it was discovered who he was, huge crowds lined the streets for his funeral.

Malaga-born **Pablo Picasso** (1881–1973) lived in Barcelona from the age of 14 until he was 23. He is said to have considered himself more Catalan than Andalucian and even after he moved to Paris in 1904 he continued to visit Barcelona regularly until the Civil War curtailed his trips. The Museu Picasso (➤ 44) is rich in art works from his Barcelona stay.

STYLE, STYLE, STYLE

● In Barcelona and throughout Catalunya there is a huge emphasis on visual style. Architecture here is innovative and daring, interior design cutting-edge, graphics and every aspect of fashion of enormous importance. You'll be aware of this through everything from shop window displays to posters and the decoration of construction scaffolding, a Barcelonan blast of colour, shape, and visual rhythm.

Top: *Parc de la Ciutadella*
Bottom: *Port Vell Aquarium*
Right: *Barceloneta*
Opposite page:
Top: *Passion facade, Sagrada Familia*
Bottom & Right: *Sagrada Familia*

city. Barcelona can be crowded in season, but it's large enough for you to escape the crowds and make your own discoveries away from the big draws. You can plan ahead, or simply enjoy wandering through the different *barris* of the city.

It's easy too, to escape the city altogether and head out for a taste of Catalunya, just as many locals do. You might simply be drawn to the coast for a day on the beach; good travel links bring historic cities and resorts like Girona and Sitges within easy reach. Or you could venture inland for a glimpse of the high Sierras behind

MODERNISME

• *Modernisme* is the Catalan version of the international movement in art and design known as art nouveau, Jugendstil, Liberty, and Secession. Barcelona's claim to pre-eminence is based on the extraordinary number of buildings erected around the turn of the 19th century by immensely talented and original architects. Their designs were heavily influenced by Moorish and Gothic architecture, but also embraced the building potential of the new industrial technologies. The fusion of the latter with organic forms reflecting the beauty of the natural world, produced a unique and innovative style.

the dramatically-sited ancient shrine of Montserrat. Some visitors even prefer to lodge outside the city along the coast, coming in daily to explore.

Wherever you are based and wherever you go, you'll be very aware of local people and their way of life. The Catalans are the first to say they are Catalan rather than Spanish, a people proud of their language and cultural heritage. Having been outlawed during the Franco years, Catalan is again the official language, with all public information in Catalan, a Romance language with links to both French and Spanish. If you speak Spanish, don't despair—most people also speak Castilian. They also know how to work hard and how to enjoy themselves. There's always time for coffee, a drink, a snack; always time to stroll and shop; and above all, time to talk for hours on end. Like other Spanish cities, Barcelona is a whole different place after dark, with what seems like the entire population out enjoying itself until late, late, late.

Go with the flow, soak it all up, and pick and choose, from the wonderful diversity of the city.

VITAL STATISTICS

● Barcelona is the second largest city in Spain, marginally smaller than Madrid.

● The city produces 20 percent of Spain's industrial output.

● More than 8 million overnight stays are made by visitors to the city each year.

● The city has a population of 1.5 million (3 million in the metropolitan area). In 1850 the population was just 235,000.

Barcelona Then

BEFORE 1000

Barcelona's origins date back to 27BC–AD14, when the Romans founded Barcino during the reign of Emperor Augustus. City walls were built in the late 3rd/early 4th century, as a result of attacks by Franks and Alemanni. AD415 saw a Visigothic invasion and the establishment of the Kingdom of Tolosa, predecessor of Catalonia. Arabs invaded in 717 and the city became Barjelunah. In 876 the Franks gained control.

FOR *EIXAMPLE*

In 1859 officials approved a plan for the *Eixample*, the grandiose extension of Barcelona beyond the city walls. The plan was finally developed in the late 19th and early 20th century, with many *modernista* buildings.

988 Catalonia becomes independent after the Franks decline to send support against the Moors.

1131–62 Ramon Berenguer IV reigns and the union of Catalonia and Aragon takes place. Barcelona becomes a major trading city.

1213–76 Jaume I reigns, and conquers Valencia, Ibiza, and Mallorca from the Moors. New city walls are built.

1354 The legislative council of Catalonia—the Corts Catalans—sets up the Generalitat to control city finances.

1410 The last ruler of the House of Barcelona, Martí I, dies without an heir. Catalonia is now ruled from Madrid, which becomes more interested in transatlantic ventures than the stagnant trade of the Mediterranean.

1462–73 The Catalan civil war rages and the economy deteriorates.

1640 Els Segadors (the Reapers) revolt against Castilian rule.

1714 Barcelona is defeated by French and Spanish troops in the War of the Spanish Succession. Catalonia becomes a province of Spain.

1813 Napoleonic troops depart. Textile manufacturing leads to a growth in the city's industry and population.

1888 The Universal Exhibition attracts 2 million visitors.

1909 Churches and convents are set aflame during the *Setmana Tràgica* (Tragic Week).

1914–18 Barcelona's economy is boosted by Spanish neutrality in World War I.

1931 The Catalan Republic is declared after the exile of King Alfonso XIII.

1939 Barcelona falls to the Nationalists, led by General Franco. Spain remains neutral during World War II.

1975 Franco dies. The restoration of the monarchy under Joan Carlos I allows the re-establishment of the Generalitat as the parliament of an autonomous regional goverment of Catalonia.

1992 Barcelona hosts the Olympic Games.

2002 *Any Internacional Gaudí* celebrates the 150th anniversary of Gaudí's birth.

2004 Barcelona hosts the UNESCO Universal Forum of Cultures.

Above (left to right): *Roderic, last king of the Visigoths; the battle of Tolosa; Columbus in Barcelona; the Siege of Barcelona; Franco and soldiers of the Nationalist Forces*

FRANCO

In 1936 armed workers in Barcelona defeated an army uprising led by Nationalist General Franco. But resistance to Franco was weakened by internal strife between Communists and Anarchists. In 1939 Barcelona fell to the Nationalists. Catalan identity and culture were crushed during the subsequent Franco dictatorship. The Catalan language was banned and the region suffered economic decline. Franco died in 1975 and the monarchy was restored.

Time to Shop

WHERE TO SHOP

There are plenty of malls and department stores—some downtown (notably in Eixample and around the Plaça de Catalunya), others further out near the ring roads. Individual, often quirky, shops are clustered mainly around the Barri Gòtic, the Raval, and La Ribera. Head for Gràcia and the Eixample for high fashion, stylish bookstores, art shops, and antique dealers. Weekly art and antique markets are held in the old city and the Port Vell. The biggest and best flea market is Els Encants (⊠ Plaça de la Glories ⊟ Glories).

Rich and stylish, as attractive to locals and Spaniards from outside Catalunya as it is to foreigners, the city rates as Spain's number one shopping destination after Madrid. The contrast between tiny, old-world, specialist shops and the glittering bastions of 21st-century retail therapy is striking; shops vary from the ultra-modern to relics from the past—an equation that makes a shopping spree serendipitous indeed.

Branches of some of Spain and Europe's best-known fashion sources are here, as well as haunts for urban trendies which stock classy and coquettish clothes with a twist. Added to that there's a wealth of serious, well-priced leather goods—shoes of every style and colour, bags of all descriptions, and deliciously supple belts, gloves, and purses. As for souvenirs of this city of Gaudì, look for useful items with a *modernisme* theme—calendars and art books, vibrant ceramics, and porcelain. The textiles are inspired; you can pick up gorgeous throws and fabrics in seductive colours and textures both from specialist shops and from the workshops where they are made.

For those who find the temptation of a designer bargain irresistible, a visit to the La Roca

Company Stores will probably be essential. Just 30 minutes drive from Barcelona are exciting top brands at discounted prices, all in a pretty, 19th-century Catalan village.

Edible gifts are always popular; the Spanish speciality, *turrón* (nougat), almonds, and olives spring to mind. For something more original head for the Boqueria market. Here you'll find items such as strings of dried peppers, aromatic honey, golden threads of saffron, sheets of dried cod, superb hams, and wonderful cheeses. Spanish nuts and dried fruits are superb—you could even take home the ingredients for a Catalan dish.

The old city is the home of Barcelona's best specialist shops. Trawling through the narrow streets of the Barri Gòtic and Raval you'll come across tiny shops devoted to wonderfully esoteric merchandise. There's even a shop devoted entirely to feathers. If you fancy a silk shawl, *mantilla*, or intricate fan you'll find it here, as well as deliciously scented candles, flamenco dresses, traditionally made perfumes, soaps, and cosmetics. The window displays are often as beautiful as the goods inside, and the tiniest item makes a wonderful gift.

Above (left to right):
*Colourful Spanish fans;
Plaça Reial's Sunday stamp
and coin market; shoppers in
Barcelona; Plaza del Rei
antique shop*

THE RAVAL

Along the narrow streets of the Raval, west of the Ramblas, you will find some of Barcelona's most interesting, and one-of-a-kind, shops. This is the place to hunt down red-hot design, second-hand fashion, clubwear, and dance accessories. Look especially on and around Calle Riera Baixa, which is also home to a Saturday alternative street market.

19

Out and About

INFORMATION

Bus Turístic
City centre stops: ✚ H8
✉ Plaça de Catalunya
✚ H7 ✉ Passeig de
Gràcia–La Pedrera
✚ F5 ✉ Francèsc
Macia–Diagonal
🕐 Daily, every 20
minutes or less. Full tour
3–4 hours.
💷 Inexpensive
Julià Tours
✉ Ronda Universitat
☎ 93 317 64 54
Pullmantur
✉ Gran Via de les Corts
Catalanes 635
☎ 93 317 12 97
Barcelona Guide Bureau
✉ Via Laietana 54
☎ 93 268 24 22
City Guides BCN
✉ Ronda Universitat 21
☎ 93 412 06 74

ORGANIZED SIGHTSEEING

Easily the best bargain in city sightseeing is the Bus Turístic, which has two routes, one running north of the city (red) and the other south (blue). One- and two-day tickets, sold on board, entitle you to discounts on the Tramvia Blau, the

Montjuïc funicular, and the harbour pleasure boats, as well as sights like the Poble Espanyol (► 31). Julià Tours and Pullmantur offer half- and full-day bus tours to principal sights. Various organizations provide individual guides, who can give you a more personal introduction to Barcelona.

EXCURSIONS
MONTSERRAT

INFORMATION

MONTSERRAT
Distance 31 miles west
Journey Time 1.5 hours
🚂 Train from Plaça
d'Espanya then cable car
✉ Monestir
☎ 93 877 77 01
🕐 Basilica 7AM–7.30PM
💷 Basilica free; museum
inexpensive

Crowds climb Montserrat ("saw-tooth mountain") to venerate the medieval statue of Our Lady of Montserrat, patron saint of Catalonia. Known as the Black Virgin because of the colour of her face, she is displayed above the altar of the church of the Monestir de Montserrat. This spectacularly sited complex, founded in 1025 and much rebuilt since then, is still home to monks and has accommodation for pilgrims. The church is most crowded at 1PM and 6.45PM daily, and at midday on Sunday, when it is filled with the voices of the monastery's boys' choir. Escape the throngs by taking a funicular and walking to the hermitage of Sant Joan, or by visiting the Santa Cova cave.

SITGES

This old town is among the most attractive of the seaside resorts on either side of Barcelona. Its fine beaches are separated by a low promontory dominated by the parish church. From the mid-19th century, Sitges attracted artists and their

hangers-on; the one who left the most lasting impact was the *modernista* painter Santiago Rusinyol, whose villa, the Cau Ferrat, is now a museum. It is filled with the magical mixture of objects with which he surrounded himself—including paintings by Pablo Picasso. Sitges has two other museums, the Palau Mar i Cel and the Museu Romàntic, which shows how life was lived by the mid-19th-century rich. The town's somewhat bohemian past gives it a raffish air that has made it popular today with gay travellers.

GIRONA

This provincial capital rising over the Onyar river is one of Catalonia's most fascinating historic towns. Its position on the main road from the French frontier made it the subject of many sieges and accounts for its sturdy walls. Supreme among Girona's several fine churches is the cathedral, whose imposing steps and baroque front conceal a fine medieval interior and Europe's widest Gothic vault. The Banys Arabs, the 13th-century baths probably designed by Moorish craftsmen, are a counterpoint to the old Jewish Quarter, the Call.

INFORMATION

SITGES
Distance 25 miles southwest
Journey Time 30–40 minutes
🚆 Train from Passeig de Gràcia or Sants stations
☎ RENFE 902 240 202
🛈 Sinea Morera, Sitges
    ☎ 93 811 76 30

Left: *Poble Espanyol*
Right: *Palau Mar i Cel at Sitges*

INFORMATION

GIRONA
Distance 62 miles northeast
Journey Time 1 hour 15 minutes
🚆 Train from Passeig de Gràcia or Sants stations
🛈 Rambla de la Llibertad 1, Girona
    ☎ 972 22 65 75

21

Walks

INFORMATION

Distance 1.2 miles
Time 1 hour (including museum visit)
Start point
★ Plaça Joan Carles I
🚇 H6 🚇 Diagonal
End point Plaça de Catalunya
🚇 H8 🚇 Catalunya
🍴 The top-floor cafeteria of the department store El Corte Inglès (✉ Plaça de Catalunya) makes an excellent vantage point for lunch
ℹ To get more from the walk, use the Patronat de Turisme's free brochure *Barcelona: Quadrat d'Or*

THE EIXAMPLE

The first part of this walk assumes you have already seen the Casa Milà (► 34) and the Manzana de la Discòrdia (► 35), and leads you past some of the lesser-known *modernista* buildings of the Eixample.

Cutting a 45-degree swathe through the grid of the Eixample is the immensely long boulevard aptly named the Diagonal. Plaça Joan Carles I, the important intersection with Passeig de Gràcia, celebrates the role of King Juan Carlos in suppressing the 1981 army *coup d'état*.

Walk eastward along the Diagonal and turn right onto Carrer Roger de Llúria, then left onto Carrer València. Both the church and the market of La Concepció arrived here in the late 19th century, the medieval church brought piece by piece from its original site in the old town.

Go west along Carrer Aragó. The crossing with Passeig de Gràcia gives you another chance to admire the extravagances of the Manzana de la Discòrdia and to make a quick visit to the Museu del Perfum. Stay on the south side of Aragó to see the rooftop sculpture of the Fundació Tàpies. Turn left to follow the central pedestrian promenade of Rambla de Catalunya to Plaça de Catalunya.

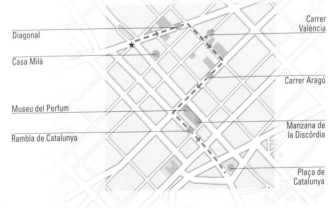

Diagonal

Carrer València

Casa Milà

Carrer Aragó

Museu del Perfum

Manzana de la Discòrdia

Rambla de Catalunya

Plaça de Catalunya

BARRI GÒTIC

This walk takes you through the old streets of the Barri Gòtic to Parc de la Ciutadella.

Carrer Rivadeneyra leads from Plaça de Catalunya via a courtyard into Carrer Santa Anna, a typical street of the Barri Gòtic. Continue along Carrer Comtal and cross Via Laietana to the Palau de la Música Catalana. Continue along Sant Pere Més Alt to the Plaça Sant Pere, with its pretty church, before going south to the Plaça Sant Augusti Vell. Find your way down Carrer Carders and then on to Carrer de Montcada, perhaps the city's finest remaining medieval street, home to the Picasso Museum. Come back and turn right onto Carrer Carders, continuing along Carrer Portal Nou to reach the approach to the Parc de la Ciutadella, dominated by the Arc de Triomf, built for the 1888 Expo. Opposite is the grandiose Palau de Justícia.

On the far side of Passeig de Pujades is the park itself. The formally laid-out area to the right has the Zoological Museum and Hivernacle greenhouse. To the left is the lake and the Great Cascade. Leave the park by the exit for Avinguda Marquès de l'Argentera, passing the grand França railway station.

INFORMATION

Distance 2 miles
Time 2 hours
Start point
★ Plaça de Catalunya
🚇 H8
🚈 Catalunya
End point Santa Maria del Mar
🚇 H9
🚈 Barceloneta
🍴 Santa Maria del Mar is surrounded by excellent bars

Palau de la Música Catalana

Plaça Sant Pere

Arc de Triomf

Palau de Justícia

Plaça Sant Augusti Vell

Zoological Museum

Picasso Museum

Parc de la Ciutadella

França Railway Station

Barcelona by Night

Left: *the Columbus Monument*
Centre: *café beneath the towering Sagrada Familia*
Right: *towards Plaça d'Espanya*

PICK OF THE PANORAMAS

From the slopes of Tibidabo, the huge peak towering behind the city, there are stupendous views over the whole city to the sea, and the area is well-endowed with bars and cafés. The mountain's name comes from the Latin *tibi dabo*—"to thee I give", the words used by the Devil when tempting Christ. Another great view can be had from Montjüic, where there are green spaces to enjoy on hot summer evenings. You could take the *teleféric* up to the castle for a bird's-eye view over the hill and the port below.

EVENING STROLLS

No matter where in Barcelona you are staying, the Rambla (► 37), the perfect place to stroll, pause, and relax, acts like a magnet for an evening *paseo*. Amble up and down its length a couple of times, then grab a table at one of the many cafés and watch the world go by. Alternatively, start at the somewhat seedily elegant Plaça Reial (► 58) nearby. Other pleasant areas to stroll include the waterfront and Port Vell (► 46), particularly agreeable in summer, and the Eixample for its wide boulevards, most notably the Passeig de Gràcia and the Rambla Catalunya. The streets of the Barri Gòtic are also atmospheric.

MUSIC, THEATRE, DANCE, AND FILM

Barcelona has a good year-round schedule of cultural evening events. The choice is wide, with everything from opera, orchestral concerts, theatre, and original language films to jazz, flamenco, and Latin American music. You can get information in the weekly entertainment guide *Guia del Ocio* and from the Virreina Cultural Information Centre on the Rambla (☎ 93 301 77 75), or call the 010 information line, where an English-speaking operator will help.

CLUBBING THE NIGHT AWAY

Barcelona is a clubber's paradise, with frequent visits from internationally famous DJs, plenty of homegrown talent, and a constantly evolving scene. Clubs and bars open and close frequently so pick up flyers and check the listings sections in *Barcelona Metropolitan* and *Punto H.*

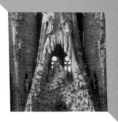

BARCELONA's
top 25 sights

The sights are shown on the maps on the inside front cover and inside back cover, numbered **1**–**25** across the city

Palau de Pedralbes

Gardens

- Gaudí's lodge with dragon gate (on C F Primo de Rivera)
- Garden pools and fountains
- Forecourt statue of Queen Isabel II

Museums

- Medieval Mudejar ware
- Ceramic works by Miró and Picasso
- *Modernista* bed of 1908
- Art deco glass
- 1930–90 Industrial Design Collection

Relaxing in the palace grounds

INFORMATION

- ✚ D4; locator map A2
- ✉ Avinguda Diagonal 686
- ☎ 93 280 50 24
- 🕐 Tue–Sat 10–6, Sun 10–3
- 🍴 Palau Reial
- 🚊 7, 33, 67, 68, 74, 75
- ♿ Good
- 🎟 Moderate; gardens free (ticket admits to both museums)
- ↔ Museu Monestir de Pedralbes (➤ 27)

When Spanish royals opened the 1888 Expo, bourgeois Barcelona had to lodge them unceremoniously in the town hall. By the time of the second Expo in 1929, the king was able to stay in this fine villa in luxuriant gardens.

Preparing a palace The city fathers' solution to the lack of a proper palace was engineered by J. A. Güell, son of architect Gaudí's great patron. The grounds of the family's villa in suburban Pedralbes already had a Gaudí gatehouse. In the 1920s, wings were added to the villa, giving it something of the look of a royal palace and the gardens were lavishly landscaped—all in time for King Alfonso's first visit in 1926. The ill-fated monarch came again, in 1929, to participate in the grand opening of the Expo, but with the proclamation of the Spanish Republic in 1931, the palace became city property. During Franco's rule, it was visited no fewer than 14 times by the dictator, who loved the finer things in life. The Generalissimo left no trace of his presence, but a pair of grand thrones grace the otherwise empty Throne Room.

Ceramics and decorative arts The palace was opened to the public in 1960 and is now the splendid setting for a couple of fascinating museums. The superlative collection of the Museu de Ceràmica explores the substantial Spanish contribution to the craft since the 12th century. The displays of the Museu de les Arts Decoratives make a wonderful introduction to the evolution of the decorative arts from the early Middle Ages onwards. The 20th-century exhibits, encompassing the eras of *Modernisme* to Minimalism, are ample evidence of Barcelona's claims to pre-eminence in design.

Museu Monestir de Pedralbes

Only a bus ride away from the bustle of central Barcelona stands this serene seat of contemplation, one of Europe's best-preserved and most atmospheric medieval monasteries. It has an intriguing musum of monastic life.

Interior of the Church of Monestir de Pedralbes

Monastic museum Once a foothill village outside Barcelona, Pedralbes still exudes a rustic atmosphere, with a cobbled street leading steeply upward to the fortress-like walls of the great monastery. The nuns first came here in the 14th century and their successors still worship in the austere church. They have had a new residence since 1983, and the historic parts of the monastery have become a fascinating museum of monastic life. The building contains numerous works of art, liturgical objects and furniture that the resident nuns accumulated over the centuries. The core of the establishment is the superb Gothic cloister, three storeys high, with elegant columns and capitals. In the centre are palms, orange trees, and cypresses; around it are the spaces that once housed varied community activities. The simple cells contrast with the grandeur of the refectory with its vaulted ceiling, and you'll see a pharmacy, an infirmary, the kitchens, the basement storerooms, and the great cistern. The chapter house has many mementos of monastic life, including the funereal urn of Sobirana de Olzet, the first abbess.

The Church of Pedrables The nuns still worship in Gothic church next to the monestry and the sounds of their vespers are often heard in the street outside. A popular place for locals to tie the knot, it is said that if the bride brings the nuns a dozen eggs the day before the ceremony it won't rain on her wedding day.

HIGHLIGHTS

Monastery
● Chapel of San Miguel, with 14th-century paintings by Spanish painter and miniaturist, Ferrer Bassa
● Tomb of Queen Elisenda, the monastery's founder
● Dioramas of the *Life of Christ* by Joan Mari

INFORMATION

✚ D3; locator map A2
✉ Baixada del Monestir 9
☎ Monastery 93 203 92 82
🕐 Tue–Sun 10–2
🚇 Reina Elisenda
🚌 22, 63, 64, 78
♿ Good
🎫 Moderate, free first Sunday of month (combined tickets with the Museu d'Història de la Ciutat)

Gràcia

Colourful facade on the Plaça del Sol

Barcelona's most distinctive suburb is not only the site of the Parc Güell and a genuine masterpiece from Gaudí. You'll also find peaceful squares, the liveliest bars, and a nine-day street party that attracts more than 2 million each year.

Cultural village From its origins as a collection of tiny farms serving three convents, Gràcia grew rapidly in the 19th century, becoming part of Barcelona itself in 1897. Gràcia was renowned then as a cultural and political centre, a stronghold of republicanism and liberalism, and this is reflected in some street names—Mercat de la Llibertat and Plaça de la Revolució. It was also a place where music and theatre thrived and today there are exhibition centres, music societies, and cultural spaces of all kinds.

Graceful Gràcia Apart from the Parc Güell, the pick of Gràcia attractions are Gaudí's exquisite Casa Vicens (► 54), one of the world's first *modernista* buildings, and Lluís Domènech i Montaner's Casa Fuster (► 54). *Plaças* such as Virreina, Sol, and Rius i Taulet are attractive places to pause for thought or stop for a coffee during the day. Boasting some of the best bars and restaurants in the city, Gràcia comes into its own at night.

Summer festival The *Festa Major* has taken place annually for more than 150 years. For nine days during the second half of August, it completely takes over Gràcia. Each street puts up a display, with themes ranging from the Wild West to the Civil War, and the suburb is a riot of colour. You'll also find music, theatre, and films, shown on a giant screen on the Plaça Diamant. The atmosphere is wonderful, and it sometimes seems the whole of Barcelona is here.

Parc Güell

Surrealist Salvador Dalí was filled with "unforgettable anguish" as he strolled among the uncanny architectural forms of this hilltop park, Antonio Gaudí's extraordinary piece of landscape design.

Unfulfilled intentions The rocky ridge, which has a magnificent prospect of Barcelona and the Mediterranean, was bought in 1895 by Gaudí's rich patron, Eusebi Güell, with the idea of developing an English-style garden city. The project flopped; only three houses of the proposed 60 were built, and the area was taken over by the city council as a park in 1923.

Anatomy of a park The main feature is the great terrace, supported on a forest of neo-Grecian columns and bounded by a sinuous balustrade-cum-bench whose form was allegedly copied from the imprint left by a human body in a bed of plaster; the surface is covered by fragments of coloured ceramic tiles. The strange space beneath the terrace was intended to be a market; it gapes cavern-like at the top of the steps leading from the park's main entrance.

Surreal landscape A ceramic serpent (or perhaps a dragon) slithers down the stairway towards the main entrance, which is guarded by two gingerbread-style buildings with bulbous roofs that must be among Gaudí's oddest creations. Gaudí scattered the park with other idiosyncratic details, steps, and serpentine paths. He lived in the house built by his pupil Berenguer, now the Casa Museu Gaudí.

HIGHLIGHTS

- Boundary wall with ceramic lettering
- Ironwork of entrance gates
- Swelling forms of vaults beneath terrace
- Palm like stonework of buttresses
- Leaning pillars of arcade
- *Modernista* furnishings in Casa Museu Gaudí

INFORMATION

- ✚ J4; locator map C1
- ✉ Carrer d'Olot
- ☎ 93 213 04 88
- ⏰ May–Aug: daily 9–9. Apr and Sep: daily 9–8. Mar and Oct: daily 9–7. Nov–Feb: daily 9–6
- 🍴 Café
- 🚉 Vallcarca (and uphill walk)
- 🚌 24, 87
- ♿ Few
- 🎟 Free

Detail from the Dragon Fountain on the entrance steps

29

Montjuïc

Covering an area bigger than the Barri Gòtic, "Jove's mountain" rises imposingly over the harbour. This is the city's finest park, a unique blend of exotic gardens and tourist attractions, including two of the city's finest museums.

Ancient beginnings Prehistoric people had settled here, high above the harbour, long before the Romans built their shrine to Jove, and the hill's quarries were the source of stone from which half the old city was built. Montjuïc has also always been a place of burial: ancient Jewish cemeteries began a custom of building elaborate tombs, still represented today in the vast Cimenteri del Sud-est on the hill's far flank. Crowning the summit is the castle, which now houses a military museum.

Panoramic views of the city from Montjuïc's cable cars

The 1929 Expo Montjuïc really came into its own in the 20th century. The Expo was preceded by a long period of preparation in which the mountain's slopes were terraced and planted to create the luxuriant landscape that exists today. Exhibition buildings were put up in a variety of styles ranging from the pompous Palau Nacional (➤ 32) to one of the key works of modern architecture, the Germany Pavilion by Mies van der Rohe (➤ 55). One of the Expo's main attractions was the Poble Espanyol and the great City Stadium was second only to London's Wembley in size. When the Olympic Games came to Barcelona in 1992, Montjuïc became Mount Olympus; the Anella Olímpica (Olympic Ring) includes the splendidly restored stadium as well as its space-age neighbour, the flying-saucer-like Palau de Sant Jordi by Japanese architect Arata Isozaki.

HIGHLIGHTS

Buildings and structures
- Fundació Joan Miró (➤ 33)
- Magic fountains (Plaça Carlos Buigas)
- Venetian towers and monumental approach to Palau Nacional

Gardens
- Parc del Fossar de la Pedrera (➤ 56)
- Mossen Costa I Llobera gardens
- Mossen Jacint Verdaguer gardens
- Teatre Grec amphitheatre

INFORMATION

➕ C9, D8/9/10, E8/9/10, F9/10; locator map C4
🍴 Several restaurants and cafés
Ⓜ Espanya
🚌 13, 61, 50, 55
↔ Poble Espanyol (➤ 31)

Poble Espanyol

Barcelona's "Spanish Village" provides a whistle-stop tour of the country's architecture and urban scenery. Thousands of tourists crowd here every year to enjoy a trip around the country in a single afternoon.

Virtual reality The Poble Espanyol was one of the star sights of the 1929 Expo, a stunning re-creation of the charm and diversity of Spanish regional architecture. Here are buildings from all the different areas of the country, faithfully re-created by dedicated architects, artists, and craftspeople. What might have turned out to be a tacky theme-park experience was so sensitively designed that it has survived, and attracts streams of visitors to this day.

Streets and squares General Primo de Rivera, who was in power during the 1929 Expo, was fanatic about Spanish unity. The Poble Espanyol, a celebration of the rich heritage of the nation as a whole, reflects his vision. It is hard to believe that the entire village, with its perimeter walls, six squares, and 2 miles of streets, was built in just a year. Virtually every style of regional building is represented and blended into a harmonious townscape, from the severe granite structures of rain-swept Galicia, to Mallorcan mansions and the sunny patios of Andalucia. Everywhere there are delightfully photogenic compositions. The village enjoys a life of its own; many buildings house working craftspeople, shops, cafés, and restaurants, and great efforts have been made to encourage nightlife. Noon on Sundays sees the main square filled with giants, clowns, puppets—and the children and parents who flock to see them.

HIGHLIGHTS

- Round towers of the Avila Gate
- Ayuntamiento (Town Hall) of Valderrobres in Plaça Mayor
- Santiago stairway
- House from Corella on Plaça Aragonesa
- Mudejar church tower from Utebo
- Church facade from Alcaniz

INFORMATION

- ✚ D/E8; locator map C4
- ✉ Marquès de Comillas s/n
- ☎ 93 325 78 66; www.poble-espanyol.com
- ◷ Sun 9–midnight; Mon 9–8; Fri–Sat 9–4AM; Tue–Thu 9–2AM
- ⅋ Restaurants, bars, cafés
- Ⓔ Espanya ⬛ 13, 50, 61
- ♿ Few
- 💲 Expensive
- ↔ Montjuïc (▶ 30)

Evocative Poble Espanyol

Museu Nacional d'Art de Catalunya

HIGHLIGHTS

- *Stoning of St. Stephen* from Sant Joan de Boi (Section 2)
- Wood-carving of Christ of Cerdanya (Section 2)
- Tost Canopy (painting on wood, Section 4)
- Carving of Calvary of Trago de Noguera (Section 4)
- *Christ in Majesty* from Sant Climent de Taüll (Section 5)
- Voussoir from Ripoll (Section 6)
- Carvings of Madonna and Child (Section 8)
- Carving of Christ in Majesty from Battló (Section 8)
- *Saints in Torment* (Section 10)

Vibrant detail from the Tost Canopy

INFORMATION

www.mnac.es

- ➕ E8; locator map C4
- ✉ Palau Nacional, Parc de Montjuïc
- ☎ 93 622 03 76
- ⏱ Tue–Sat 10–7; Sun and hols 10–2.30
- 🚇 Espanya 🚌 13, 61
- ♿ Excellent 💶 Moderate
- ↔ Montjuïc (▶ 30)

The impressive Palau Nacional, which dominates the northern flank of Montjuïc, houses the National Museum of Catalunyan Art. The Romanesque collection is a fascinating testament to the region's rich history.

Romanesque riches The climb from Plaça d'Espanya is less formidable than it seems; there are escalators in addition to the steps. Even if there weren't, the art treasures in the Palace would be worth the walk. Catalonia has an exceptionally rich heritage of Romanesque art, created as Christianity recolonized the valleys of the Pyrenees in the 12th and 13th centuries. Powerful images of Christ in Majesty, the Virgin Mary, and the saints promoted piety among a peasant population recently released from the Moorish yoke. By the early 20th century, such art enjoyed little prestige, and it was only through the heroic efforts of a dedicated band of art historians and archeologists that so much was saved from decay and theft.

National heritage The collection consists of an array of ecclesiastical treasures, sculptures, and carvings and, in an innovative renovation, spaces replicate the original environment in which the wall paintings first worked their magic. From the end of 2004, the collections previously on display at the Museu d'Art Modern in the Parc de la Ciutadella and the Thyssen-Bornemisza collection, will take up their new positions here, making this the most complete retrospective of the history of Catalan art in the world.

Fundació Joan Miró

Poised on the flank of Montjuïc is this white-walled temple to the art of Joan Miró, its calm interior spaces, patios, and terraces are an ideal setting for the works of this most Catalan of all artists.

Miró and Barcelona Born in Barcelona in 1893, Joan Miró never lost his feeling for the city and the surrounding countryside, though he spent much of the 1920s and 1930s in Paris and Mallorca. His paintings and sculptures, with their intense primary colours and swelling, dancing, and wriggling forms, are instantly recognizable, but he also gained renown for his expressive ceramics and graphic drawings inspired by political turmoil in Spain. In 1958, he designed a tiled wall for the UNESCO building in Paris. Miró's distinctive influence is visible in graphic work all over Barcelona and locals as well as tourists flock to the Foundation, which is also a cultural centre dedicated to the promotion of contemporary art. It houses changing exhibitions, concerts, a library, shops, and a café. Miró's works (10,000 in all, including 217 paintings) are complemented by those of numerous contemporaries including Balthus, Calder, Duchamp, Ernst, Léger, Matisse, and Moore.

Mediterranean masterpiece The monumental yet intimate Foundation was built in 1974 by Miró's old friend and collaborator, the architect Josep-Luis Sert, in a style that remains modern, yet traditionally Mediterranean in its use of forms such as domes, arches, and roof and floor tiles. It sits easily in the landscape, and its interpenetrating spaces even incorporate old trees like the ancient olive in one of the courtyards. There are glorious views over the city, especially from the roof terrace.

Striking tapestry from the Fundació Miró

HIGHLIGHTS

- Painting, *The Morning Star*, dedicated to Miró's widow
- *Personage* (1931)
- Surrealist *Man and Woman in front of a pile of excrements* (1935)
- Barcelona Series (1939–44) Civil War graphics
- Anthropomorphic sculptures on roof terrace
- *Tapis de la Fundació* tapestry (1979)

INFORMATION

www.bcn.fjmiro.es

- E9; locator map D4
- Parc de Montjuïc
- 93 443 94 70
- Jul–Sep: Tue–Sat 10–8 (Thu 10–9.30); Sun and hols 10–2.30. Oct–Jun: Tue–Sat 10–7 (Thu 10–9.30); Sun and hols 10–2.30
- Café-restaurant
- Espanya 61
- Montjuïc funicular from Paral.lel Metro
- Good Moderate
- Book and gift shop
- Montjuïc (➤ 30)

33

Casa Milà

HIGHLIGHTS

- Ground floor entrance with wall and ceiling paintings

Espai Gaudí
- Audio-visual show
- Plans and models of major buildings
- Stereofunicular model of building structure
- Gaudí souvenir shop (separate entrance)
- Exhibition space of the Fundació Caixa de Catalunya

INFORMATION

- H6; locator map D2
- Passeig de Gràcia 92
- 93 484 59 00
- Daily 10–8
- Diagonal
- 7, 16, 17, 22, 24, 28
- Good (but not on roof)
- Expensive
- Manzana de la Discòrdia (► 35)

Surreal chimneys from the Casa Milà

"Get a violin" was architect Gaudí's response to a resident who wondered where to install a grand piano in this coral reef of an apartment block, which seems designed for slithering sea creatures rather than human beings.

The grotto of the Passeig de Gràcia Anecdotes about the Casa Milà abound: the artist Santiago Rusinyol is supposed to have said that a snake would be a more suitable pet here than a dog. Lampooned for decades after its completion in 1912, this extraordinary building has been rescued from neglect and opened to visitors. Nicknamed La Pedrera (stone quarry), it was built for Pere Milà Camps, a rich dandy who afterwards complained that Gaudí's extravagance had reduced him to penury. The steel frame that supports the seven-floor structure is completely concealed behind an undulating outer skin of stone bedecked with balconies whose encrustations of ironwork resemble floating fronds of seaweed. Obscured from the street, the rooftop undulates too, and in rain and high winds gives a good impression of a ship in a stormy sea.

One of Gaudí's greatest Gaudí originally proposed a spiral ramp that would bring automobiles to the apartment doors—an impractical idea as it turned out—but the Casa Milà nevertheless had one of the world's first underground garages. The building's beautifully brick-vaulted attics have become the Espai Gaudí, the best place to learn about Gaudí's work. **Ruta del Modernisme** tickets give discounts for the main modernist sites

- Passeig de Gràcia 41
- 93 488 01 39.

Manzana de la Discòrdia

A century ago, the bourgeoisie of Barcelona vied with each other in commissioning ever more extravagant apartment blocks. The most extraordinary of these ornament the Block of Discord on Passeig de Gràcia.

Enlivening the Eixample In an attempt to relieve the rigidity of Cerdà's grid of streets, *modernista* architects studded the Eixample with some of the most exciting urban buildings ever seen. *Modernisme*, the uniquely Catalan contribution to late 19th-century architecture (► 14, 54), has obvious links with art nouveau, but here it also breathes the spirit of nationalism and civic pride because Barcelona was the richest city in Spain. The Manzana de la Discòrdia juxtaposes the work of three great architects of the age.

No. 35 Domènech i Montaner completed the six-storey Casa Lleó-Morera in 1905. Much of the interior and exterior of this corner building was destroyed during improvements in the 1940s, but its striking *modernista* style and curved balconies have survived.

No. 41 Built in 1898 by Puig i Cadafalch, the Casa Amatller has an internal courtyard and staircase like the medieval palaces along Carrer Montcada. Outside, it is a wonderful mixture of Catalan Gothic and Flemish Renaissance, faced with coloured tiles and topped by a big gable.

No. 43 The Casa Batlló reflects the hand of Antoni Gaudí, who remodelled the house in 1906. It is said to represent the triumph of St. George over the dragon with its heaving roof (the dragon's back), scaly skin of mosaic tiles, windows (the bones of victims), and tower (the saint's lance).

HIGHLIGHTS

No. 35
- Exterior sculptures
- Dome perched on columns

No. 41
- Sculpture of St. George and dragon by entrance
- Grotesque sculptures in third-floor windows
- Lamps and stained-glass panels in entrance

No. 43
- Chromatic designs on facade by Gaudí's collaborator, the artist Josep Maria Jujol

INFORMATION

- ✚ H7; locator map D2
- ✉ Passeig de Gràcia 35, 41, 43
- 🕐 Casa Batlló: daily 9AM–8PM
- 🚇 Passeig de Gràcia
- 🚌 7, 16, 17, 22, 24, 28
- 🔗 Casa Milà (► 34)

Gaudí's Casa Batlló

Museu d'Art Contemporani

INFORMATION

www.cccb.org
- G8; locator map D3
- Museum, Plaça dels Angels 1; Centre, Montalegre 5
- Museum 93 412 08 10; Centre 93 481 00 69
- Museum Mon–Fri 11–7.30 (closed Tue); Sat 10–8; Sun and hols 10–3. Exhibitions at Centre Wed and Sat 11–8; Sun and hols 11–7; Tue, Thu, and Fri 11–2, 4–8
- Catalunya, Universitat
- 9, 14, 24, 38, 41, 50, 54, 55, 58, 59, 64, 66, 91, 141
- Good
- Moderate
- La Rambla (➤ 37)

Could this be Barcelona's answer to Paris's Centre Pompidou? A glittering white home for late 20th-century art, known as the MACBA, has given the run-down inner city district of Raval an ultra-modern shot in the arm.

A modern museum For many years Barcelona felt the lack of an adequate establishment devoted to the contemporary visual arts. During the repressive Franco years, the city found it difficult to keep in touch with the international avant-garde, while its own progressive artists enjoyed little official encouragement. Now two major institutions are bringing it back into the mainstream. By any reckoning, the Museum of Contemporary Art is remarkable, though its long white walls and huge size are strikingly at odds with the ramshackle, dun-coloured facades of its neighbours across the plain modern *plaça* in a less smart part of town. The shining new structure, designed by the American architect Richard Meier, opened in 1995. Its exhibition spaces lead on to a great atrium and are reached by a spectacular series of ramps and glass-floored galleries, sometimes almost upstaging the works on display. Temporary exhibitions featuring local and international artists complement the museum's own extensive collection, which is exhibited in rotation.

Centre de Cultura Contemporànea Housed in the strikingly adapted old monastery buildings of the Casa de la Caritat, the Centre for Contemporary Culture promotes a whole range of activities focused on cultural and social themes. Each year sees a season of cultural and theatrical events exploring different aspects of contemporary art and style, from fashion and architecture to modern communications.

La Rambla

Supreme among city strolling spaces, the Rambla stretches seductively from Plaça de Catalunya to the waterfront. Venerable plane trees frame the broad sidewalk, which teems with activity at all hours.

Pedestrian paradise Most Catalan towns have their Rambla, a promenade where people go to see and be seen. None, however, enjoys the worldwide fame of Barcelona's. Sooner rather than later, every visitor joins the crowds along this vibrant central space, where strollers rule and traffic is confined to either side. More than a mere thoroughfare, the Rambla is a *place*—somewhere to linger, to sit, to rendezvous, to watch street entertainers, to buy a paper, to simply breathe in the essence of the city. Until the 18th century, breathing deeply was highly inadvisable; the Rambla owes its origin to an open sewer along the line of the city walls which once stood here.

More than one Rambla The Rambla changes its name several times on its way down toward the Columbus Column, just over half a mile from Plaça de Catalunya. First comes Rambla de Canaletes with its famous drinking fountain and well-stocked newsstands, then Rambla dels Estudis, named for the university once sited here. The Rambla de Sant Josep is also known as Rambla de les Flors, after its profusion of flowerstands. The halfway point is marked by Miró's colourful mosaic in the pavement and by Liceu subway station, named after the city's opera house. The Rambla dels Caputxins follows, with its cafés, then the Rambla de Santa Monica, which has retained its earthy charm despite attempts at modernization.

HIGHLIGHTS

Starting at Plaça de Catalunya
● Bird and pet market
● Baroque Betlem Church (➤ 59)
● 18th-century Palau Moja bookshop and cultural centre
● 18th-century Palau de la Virreina information centre
● La Boqueria covered market (➤ 78)
● Gran Teatre del Liceu
● Metal dragon on umbrella shop
● Centre d'Art Santa Monica
● Museu de Cera (Wax Museum) (➤ 61)

Detail from a modernista *shop front*

INFORMATION

🞣 G8/9; locator map E3
🚇 Catalunya, Liceu, Drassanes
🚌 91
🔁 Drassanes (➤ 38), Port Vell (➤ 46)

37

Drassanes & Museu Marítim

HIGHLIGHTS

- Medieval navigation charts
- Displays on 19th-century submarine *Ictíneo*
- Figurehead collection
- Fishing caravel of 1907

Great Adventure of the Sea

- Catalan Seapower in the 19th century
- Steamships and Emigration
- The Submarine World

INFORMATION

- ✛ G9; locator map E3
- ✉ Av. de les Drassanes
- ☎ 93 342 99 20
- ⏰ Daily 10–7. Closed 1 Jan, 1 May, 24 Jun, 24–25 Dec
- 🚇 Drassanes
- 🚌 14, 36, 38, 57, 59, 64, 91
- ♿ Few
- 💵 Moderate
- ↔ La Rambla (➤ 37), Port Vell (➤ 46)

Magnificent reproduction of the Galera Real

Cut off from today's harbour by cobbled docksides, the Gothic buildings of the Royal Shipyards are an evocative reminder of Barcelona's longstanding affair with the sea, as well as a unique monument to the Middle Ages.

Cathedral of the sea By the 13th century, Catalan sea power extended over much of the western Mediterranean. These ships were built in the covered Royal Shipyards, or Drassanes, a series of long parallel halls with roofs supported on high arches. The effect is of sheer grandeur—of a great cathedral rather than a functional workspace.

Ships on show The Drassanes are now a fascinating museum, displaying paintings, charts, model ships, and all kinds of maritime memorabilia as well as a number of boats. These are all upstaged by the *Galera Real*, a full-size reproduction of the galley from which Don Juan d'Austria oversaw the defeat of the Turkish navy at the Battle of Lepanto in 1571. Built to commemorate the 400th anniversary of the battle, this elegant vessel is nearly 65 feet long. The original was propelled to victory at high speed by chained galley slaves. You can see statues of some of them, along with the commander, who stands in the ornate stern, from a high catwalk, that also gives you a fair view of the building itself. Housed in a large exhibition hall, the *Galera Real* forms part of an exciting multimedia exhibit, where you can explore ships and warehouses and watch oarsmen bent over their galley oars. Through visual and acoustic effects, Catalonia's seafaring history is brought vividly to life.

Sagrada Familia

George Orwell thought Gaudí's great Temple of the Holy Family one of the ugliest buildings he ever saw, and wondered why the Anarchists hadn't wrecked it in the Civil War. Today it is an emblem of the city.

Devoted designer A must on every visitor's itinerary, Barcelona's most famous building is a mere fragment of what its architect intended. The ultra-pious Gaudí (► 13) began work in 1883, and for the latter part of his life dedicated himself utterly to building a temple that would do penance for the materialism of the modern world. There was never any expectation that the great structure would be completed in his lifetime; his plan called for 18 high towers dominated by an even taller one, an amazing 560 feet high, dedicated to Jesus Christ. What he did succeed in completing was one of the towers, the major part of the east (Nativity) front, the pinnacled apse, and the crypt, where he camped out during the last months of his life before he was run down and killed by a tram. Ever since, the fate of the building has been the subject of sometimes bitter controversy.

Work in progress Many *Barcelonins* would have preferred the church to be left as it was at Gaudí's death, a monument to its inimitable creator. This view seems to have been at least partly shared by the Anarchists during the Civil War; they destroyed Gaudí's models and drawings though they spared the building itself. But enthusiasm for completion of the project was revived in the 1950s. Work has continued, though opponents strongly believe that attempting to reproduce Gaudí's unique forms in modern materials can only lead to the creation of pastiche.

HIGHLIGHTS

- Crypt museum
- Controversial contemporary sculpture on Passion facade
- Elevator or stairway into tower (not for the fearful)
- Symbolic sculptures of Nativity facade

INFORMATION

- ✚ J6/7; locator map E1
- ✉ Plaça Sagrada Familia
- ☎ 93 207 30 31
- 🕐 Daily, Apr–Sep 9–8, Mar and Oct 9–7, Nov–Feb 9–6
- 🚇 Sagrada Familia
- 🚌 10, 19, 33, 34, 43, 44, 50, 51
- 🎫 Expensive (additional charge for elevator)

Stonework showing the Annunciation

39

Palau de la Música Catalana

HIGHLIGHTS

Main facade

- Catalan songsters in mosaic
- Composers' busts
- Corner sculpture *Allegory of Catalan Folksong*
- Foyer vaults with floral capitals
- Lluís Millet Room
- Bust of Pau (Pablo) Casals (given 1936)
- Modern statue of Millet conducting (outside new entrance)

INFORMATION

www.palaumusica.org

- H8; locator map E2
- Sant Francesc de Paula 2
- 93 295 72 00
- Telephone for guided visits, daily 10–3.30 (Jul, Aug 10–6), every 30 mins
- Bar 🚇 Urquinaona
- 17, 19, 40, 45
- Good 🔆 Moderate
- Catedral (➤ 41)

Extravagant decoration on the Palau de la Música Catalana

For nearly a century, this glittering jewel has served not only as a concert hall but also as an icon of Catalan cultural life. The profusion of ornament is staggering—a delight in itself.

Domènech's delights The sumptuous Palace of Catalan Music was designed by the great *modernista* architect Domènech i Montaner as the home of the Catalan national choir, the Orfeó. It was inaugurated in 1908 to unanimous acclaim and became a symbol of the new renaissance in Catalan culture. Montaner gave the building a steel frame to support profuse interior and exterior decoration intended to inspire and instruct. This decoration was the work of his own ceramicists, tilers, painters, glassworkers, and tilers.

Art-full auditorium Riches encrust the main facade, the entrance hall, the foyer, and staircase, but the 2,000-seat concert hall is even more ornate. Light pours in through the transparent walls and from the roof, from which hangs an extraordinary bowl of stained glass. The proscenium arch, far from being a static frame, seems to swell and move, such is the dynamism of its pale pumice sculptures. On the left, a willow tree shelters the great mid-19th-century reviver of Catalan music, Josep Anselm Clavé; on the right a bust of Beethoven is upstaged by Wagnerian Valkyries rollicking through the clouds. Equally stunning is the curving wall at the back of the stage, from which emerge the 18 Muses of music. It's worth the trouble to reserve in advance for one of the weekly concerts; apart from the splendour of the building, the acoustics are superb.

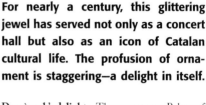

Catedral

This 14th-century cathedral is one of the finest examples of the Catalan Gothic style. It is a noble successor to its Romanesque predecessor and an even older early Christian basilica.

City church Dedicated to an early Christian virgin and martyr, Eulàlia, the cathedral stands firmly at the epicentre of city life. Weekends see people gather to dance the elegant *sardana* (▶ 62), a stately Catalan folk dance which symbolizes unity. Inside, worshippers easily outnumber tourists. The cloister is a calm refuge from the city with its magnolias, tall palms, fountain, and gaggle of geese.

Medley of styles
The cathedral was begun at the very end of the 13th century and was completed, except for the main facade, by the middle of the 15th. However, it was not until the mid-19th century that

sufficient funds had been accumulated to construct the facade—fashionable but somewhat incongruous in its French-Gothic style. You could spend hours peering at the sometimes faded treasures in the 29 chapels. The most fascinating of these is the old chapter house to the right of the main entrance; beneath a roof rising 65 feet into a star vault is the Christ of Lepanto, a life-size figure carried into the thick of the famous naval battle aboard the royal flagship (▶ 38).

HIGHLIGHTS

- Crypt with alabaster tomb of St. Eulàlia
- Late medieval and Renaissance choir stalls
- Tomb of 11th-century Ramon Berenguer I
- Museu Capitular (cathedral museum)

Cloister
- Ironwork screens of chapels
- Tomb slabs in floor
- Chapel of St. Lucia

Plaça de la Seu
- Picasso's graffiti on College of Architects building

Barcelona's cathedral in the Barri Gòtic

INFORMATION

- ✚ H9; locator map E3
- ✉ Plaça de la Seu
- ☎ 93 315 15 54
- 🕐 Daily 8–1.15, 4.30–7.30. Guided tours 1.30–4.30
- 🚇 Jaume I
- 🚌 17, 19, 40, 45
- ♿ Good
- Guided tours: moderate
- ↔ Plaça del Rei (▶ 42)
- ❓ Occasional access to tower and roof

41

Plaça del Rei

INFORMATION

- H9; locator map E3
- 93 315 11 11
- Tue–Sat 10–2, 4–8 (Jul–Sep 10–8); Sun and hols 10–3
- Jaume I
- 17, 19, 40, 45
- Poor
- Moderate. Ticket admits to museum, Roman remains, Saló del Tinell, chapel, and tower. Free for under 16s and 1st Sat of month
- Catedral (➤ 41)
- Souvenir and bookshop (entrance Carrer Llibreteria)

Nowhere in Barcelona can the antiquity of the city be experienced as intimately as in the Roman settlement of Barcino, the underground world that extends beneath the medieval palace and the Plaça del Rei.

Remains of Roman Barcelona The centre of Roman Barcelona lies in the area extending beneath Plaça Sant Jaume and Plaça del Rei, while chunks of its walls protrude in a number of other places. One of the best-preserved sections faces Plaça Ramon Berenguer el Gran, next to Plaça del Rei; above the Roman wall and towers are later layers of building, including the austere medieval Chapel of St. Agatha.

Museu d'Historia de la Ciutat The City History Museum's exhibits trace Barcelona's evolution from Roman trading post to metropolis. The museum on Plaça del Rei occupies a medieval palace moved here in 1931 when the Via Laietana was driven through the Barri Gòtic. Remains of the old Roman town were revealed by excavations carried out during the rebuilding work. Mosaic floors and parts of surrounding walls are among the underground ruins accessible from the museum. Other relics from Barcelona's history include statues and an oil press.

Regal relics Back in the Plaça del Rei, which is fairly sombre except during open-air concerts, admire the outside of the buildings that make up the medieval palace. For the real feel of the epoch, go inside, to the splendidly arched space of the 14th-century Saló del Tinell, the banqueting hall where Columbus was received on his return from the New World. Also visit the Chapel of St. Agatha and climb the five-storey lookout tower Mirador del Rei Martí, named for King Martí.

Plaça Sant Jaume

The *sardana* danced here every Sunday evening is one expression of Catalan culture; other symbols of Catalan identity are the palaces facing each other across the square, the Generalitat and the Ajuntament.

Provincial parliament The *plaça*—for centuries the site of a church and a cemetery—is one of the focal points of city life. Here demonstrations and processions wind up, and many a historic speech has been made, including the proclamation of the short-lived Catalan Republic in 1931. The Palau de la Generalitat, on the north side of the square, is the home of the regional government, successor to the Corts Catalanes of the medieval kingdom of Catalonia and Aragon. Begun in the 14th century, the building housing the Palau de la Generalitat has several features celebrating St. George, the patron saint of Catalonia; the chapel is named after him, and there's a medieval George over the 15th-century facade on Carrer Bisbe Irurita and a more modern George on the frontage overlooking the square. Generalitat has guided tours between 10.30–1.30 on 2nd and 4th Sunday of each month.

City Hall The Ajuntament or Casa de la Ciutat, the seat of city government, is more eager to show off its treasures. Beyond the 19th-century main facade, the courtyard retains the feeling of a medieval palace. Stairways lead to an open gallery off which opens the exquisite 14th-century Saló de Cent (Room of the Hundred). From here, the semi-democratic Consell de Cent (Council of the Hundred) ruled Barcelona like a city-state for nearly five centuries.

HIGHLIGHTS

Ajuntament
- Original medieval side facade
- Courtyard sculptures by Miró, Gargallo, Subirachs
- Tiles with craft implements (Saló de Cent)
- Council Chamber (off Saló de Cent)
- Mural of Catalan scenes (on stairway)
- Saló de Croniques with historical murals by Sert

Exterior of Generalitat

INFORMATION

Ajuntament
- ✚ H9; locator map E3
- ☎ 93 402 70 00
- 🕙 Sun 10–2
- Ⓜ Liceu, Jaume I
- 🚌 14, 17, 19, 38, 40, 45, 59, 91
- ♿ Good
- 💶 Free
- ↔ La Rambla (➤ 37), Plaça del Rei (➤ 42), Catedral (➤ 41)
- ❓ Concerts in the Saló de Cent

43

Museu Picasso

HIGHLIGHTS

- Ceramics from 1940s and 1950s
- *Barceloneta Beach* (1896)
- *Science and Charity* (1897)
- *La Nana* (The Dwarf), 1901
- *El Loco* (The Madman), 1904
- *Harlequin* (1917)
- *Las Meninas* suite (1957)
- Cannes paintings of landscapes and doves (late 1950s)

INFORMATION

- H9; locator map E3
- Carrer Montcada 15–19
- 93 319 63 10
- Tue–Sat and hols 10–7.30; Sun 10–2.30
- Café-restaurant
- Jaume I
- 14, 16, 17, 19, 36, 39, 40, 45, 51, 57, 59
- Good
- Expensive. Free 1st Sun of month
- Santa Maria del Mar (➤ 45)
- Large souvenir shop

Las Meninas: *detail.*
© Succession/DACS
1977

Picasso, the greatest painter of modern times, came to live in Barcelona at the age of 14. Many of his formative experiences took place in the old town, so it is appropriate that a museum devoted to his work should be here.

Picasso's palace The Picasso Museum's collection, though extensive, concentrates on certain periods of Picasso's life and artistic evolution, including his time in Barcelona. The work benefits enormously from its setting; the magnificent Palau Berenguer d'Aguilar and four adjacent buildings give an excellent idea of the lifestyle enjoyed by the rich merchant families at the height of medieval Barcelona's prosperity.

At home and away An Andalucian hailing from Malaga, Pablo Ruiz Picasso accompanied his art teacher father and family to Barcelona in 1895. He could already draw like an angel and his skills flourished at his father's academy and later, at art school in Madrid. Beginning in 1899, he immersed himself in bohemian Barcelona, frequenting the red-light district centred on Carrer d'Avinyó, the inspiration for his innovative *Demoiselles d'Avignon* (1907). He became an habitué of Els Quatre Gats (Four Cats ➤ 70–71), a café where he designed the menu as well as sketching the clientele of artists and barflies. His first exhibition was held here in 1900, the year he made his first visit to Paris. France was to be his real home after that, but he returned to Barcelona many times, and much of the work in his Blue Period (*c*1902–1904) was carried out here. The Civil War, which provoked one of his most passionate paintings, *Guernica*—now housed at the Centro Nacional de Arte Reina Sofía in Madrid—put an end to these visits.

Santa Maria del Mar

A fortress of the faith in the old port of the Ribera, the Church of Our Lady of the Sea is one of the greatest expressions of Catalan Gothic. It was built on the proceeds of Barcelona's maritime supremacy in the Middle Ages.

The Ribera Literally "the seaside" or "waterfront," the Ribera was the city's centre of gravity in the 13th century, when Catalan commerce dominated the Western Mediterranean ports. Successful merchants and entrepreneurs set themselves up in fine town houses close to the busy shore, cheek by jowl with labourers, dock porters, and craftsmen. The street names of the Ribera still reflect the trades once practiced here: Assaonadors (tanners), Espaseria (swordmaking), Argenteria (silversmithing), Sombreres (hatters).

People's Church Santa Maria was begun in 1329, the foundation stone commemorating the Catalan conquest of Sardinia. Sometimes referred to as the Cathedral of the Ribera, Santa Maria has always been a popular church, the focus of this once busy harbour district; the whole population is supposed to have toiled on its construction for 50 years. The life of the Ribera was reflected in decorative touches such as delightful depictions of dock-workers on doors and the altar. The altar is crowned by a sculpture of a 15th-century ship. Other than that, the interior of the church is almost bare; its elaborate baroque furnishings were torched during the Civil War, and now the calm and symmetry created by its high vaults and by the majestic spacing of its octagonal columns can be appreciated without distraction.

HIGHLIGHTS

Santa Maria
- Rose window in west front

In the Ribera
- Passeig del Born with central Rambla
- 19th-century glass and iron Born Market building
- Fosser de les Moreres plaza
- Medieval houses in Carrer de les Caputxes

INFORMATION

- H9; locator map E3
- Plaça de Santa Maria
- 93 310 23 90
- Daily 9.30–1.30, 4.30–8
- Jaume 1
- 14, 17, 36, 39, 45, 51, 57, 59, 64
- Good
- Free
- Museu Picasso (➤ 44)

The magnificent interior of Santa Maria del Mar

Port Vell

INFORMATION

Aquarium

✚ H10; locator map E3

✉ Moll d'Espanya

☎ 93 221 74 74

🕐 Jul–Aug: daily 9.30AM–11PM. Jun and Sep: daily 9.30AM–9.30PM. Oct–May: daily 9.30AM–9PM

🍴 Café 🚇 Drassanes

🚌 14, 17, 36, 38, 40, 45, 57, 59, 64, 91

♿ None 💲 Expensive

🔄 Drassanes (➤ 38)

Monument a Colom

✚ G9; Locator map E3

✉ Plaça del Portal de la Pau

☎ 93 302 52 24

🕐 Jun–Sep: daily 9–8.30. Apr–May: Mon–Fri 10–1.30, 3.30–7.30; Sat, Sun and hols 10–7.30. Oct–Mar: Mon–Fri 10–1.30, 3.30–6.30; Sat, Sun and hols 10–6.30

🚇 Barceloneta, Drassanes

🚌 19, 40 to Port Vell, or 14, 17, 36, 38, 40, 45, 57, 59, 64, 91

♿ Good 💲 Inexpensive

🔄 Drassanes (➤ 38), Palau de Mar (➤ 47)

Renovations in the early 1990s reclaimed the Old Port and reintegrated it into city life. The modern Rambla de Mar walkway extends across the water to the Maremagnum complex, at the heart of the Old Port.

Back to the sea Barcelona has often been accused of ignoring the sea on which so much of its prosperity depended. In the past, the closest most tourists came to it was an ascent of the 165-foot Monument a Colom, at the seaward end of the Rambla, which commemorates the return of Columbus from the New World in 1493. The port area remained unvisited. Now, the Port Vell is given over to pleasure and entertainment and most commercial activity takes place among the modern port installations to the west, although the big ferries to the Balearics still depart from here.

Peninsula The Maremagnum, a huge covered shopping and entertainment complex, at the heart of the old port, is connected to the mainland by the Rambla de Mar. This obelisk-lined walkway is usually thronged with tourists, but there are peaceful spots for a stroll. It is particularly appealing in summer, when you want a sea breeze, and at night, when checking out a couple of the clubs and bars are worth checking out. Apart from the Maremagnum's clutch of uninspiring shops and restaurants, you'll find the aquarium, which is one of the largest in Europe and requires a good couple of hours for a visit. Don't miss walking through the 265-feet-long glass tunnel—sharks are just a few inches away from your face. Also worthwhile is the IMAX movie house, which regularly screens spectacular natural history films and other movies.

Palau de Mar

Dispel any ignorance of Catalonia's past with a visit to the entertaining Palace of the Sea, home to the Museum of Catalan History. Innovative exhibits clarify what has gone into the creation of this nation within a nation.

Catalonia! Catalonia! An imposing late 19th-century warehouse, which has been expensively converted into offices and restaurants, houses this stimulating museum. Although Catalan history may be something of a closed book to casual visitors, it's worth knowing more about—the past speaks volumes about the present and current aspirations. General Franco wanted Catalan identity to disappear altogether; the museum is one of many initiatives that the regional government (the Generalitat) took to restore it. The exhibits are exclusively in Catalan, but many are self-explanatory, and Spanish and English summaries are available.

Intriguing exhibits The waterfront museum highlights themes from history in a series of spaces grouped around a central atrium. There are few artefacts on display, but exhibits are truly ingenious; you can work an Arab waterwheel, walk over a skeleton in its shallow grave, climb on to a cavalier's charger and test the weight of his armour, enter a medieval forest, peer into a primitive stone cabin, enjoy a driver's-eye view from an early tram, and cower in a Civil War air-raid shelter. Sound effects, films, and interactive screens enhance the experience.

HIGHLIGHTS

- Early ship packed with amphorae
- Moorish shop
- Sinister Civil Guards pursuing insurgents
- Civil War machine-gun emplacement
- Franco-era schoolroom
- 1930s kitchen with objects to handle
- First edition of George Orwell's *Homage to Catalonia*
- 1960s tourist bar with *Speak Inglis/Parle Frances* sign

Bronze exhibit from this innovative museum

INFORMATION

- ✚ H9/10; locator map F3
- ✉ Plaça de Pau Vila 3
- ☎ 93 225 47 00
- 🕐 Tue, Thu, Fri, Sat 10–7, Wed 10–8, Sun 10–2.30
- 🍴 Café
- Ⓜ Barceloneta
- 🚌 14, 17, 39, 40, 45, 57, 59, 64
- ♿ Good
- 💰 Moderate
- ↔ Barceloneta (➤ 49), Port Vell (➤ 46)

Parc de la Ciutadella

HIGHLIGHTS

- Hivernacle conservatory
- Umbracle conservatory

Sculptures

- *Sorrow* by Josep Llimona
- *Lady with Parasol* by Joan Roig, 1884 (in Zoo)
- Modern *Homage to the Universal Exposition of 1888*
- *Homage to Picasso* by A Tàpies (1983) (on Passeig de Picasso)

INFORMATION

- J9; locator map F2
- Arc de Triomf, Barceloneta
- 14, 39, 40, 41, 42, 51, 141
- Barceloneta (► 49), Museu Picasso (► 44), Santa Maria del Mar (► 45)

In the 1860s and 1870s the great Citadel, a longtime symbol of Bourbon oppression, was gleefully demolished. In its place, the city laid out its first public park, still a shady haven on the edge of the city centre.

The Citadel Covering an area almost as big as the city itself at the time, the monstrous Citadel was built to cow the Catalans after their defeat on 11 September, 1714, by the new Bourbon monarch of Spain, Philip V. (Paradoxically, this date has become Catalonia's national holiday). A garrison of 8,000 troops kept the population in check, and the Citadel was loathed as a place where local patriots were executed. In 1868, the Catalan General Juan Prim y Prats came to power and ensured his popularity by ordering its demolition, a process already begun by the enthusiastic citizenry.

The park today The public park that took the Citadel's place (and name) shows little trace of the great fortress, though the Arsenal now houses the Catalan Parliament. Other structures are leftovers from the Universal Expo of 1888: an ornate Arc de Triomf (Triumphal Arch), and a *modernista* café designed by Domènech i Montaner and now home to the Zoological Museum. The zoo itself is to the south (► 61). Throughout the park, fine trees and shrubs and a boating lake soften the formal layout. The imposing Font Monumental, an extraordinary fountain feature, incorporates just about every allegorical element possible beneath its own triumphal arch—Niagara Falls meets the Brandenburg Gate. Some of the extravagant iron- and rock-work is attributed to the young Antoni Gaudí.

Barceloneta

The streets of Barceloneta, cramped and flagged by flapping laundry, evoke the culture of a traditional Mediterranean seaport. Cut off from the rest of the city for years, this vibrant area has its own atmosphere and identity.

Little Barcelona Displaced by the building of the Ciutadella (▶ 48), many people from the Ribera moved, to live in shanty dwellings between the harbour and the sea. In 1751 the makeshift shacks were swept away, the land was reclaimed, and this new, triangular district, Barceloneta, was developed. Designed by a French army engineer, Prosper Verboom, it's laid out on a distictly military grid pattern, with long narrow blocks of identical housing, the regularity broken by squares. By the 19th-century the *barri* had become the traditional home of dock workers and fishermen, divided from the rest of the city after the construction of a rail and road barrier at one end.

Moves of change During the 1990s the whole of the Port Vell (▶ 46) was redeveloped and Barceloneta's Passeig Joan de Borbó, once a dockyard service road, became a smart waterfront promenade. The famous *chiringuitos*, basic but wonderful fish, paella, and seafood restaurants that once lined the beaches, were closed, the beach itself cleaned up, and another seaward facing *passeig* built to link the area with the Port Olímpic—and there are further schemes in the pipeline. Many of the *chiringuitos* have relocated to the Port Vell side, so you can still enjoy one of the freshest fish dinners in Barcelona, at restaurants which have been drawing the weekend crowds for years. Follow it up with a stroll round Barceloneta's atmospheric streets.

HIGHLIGHTS

- Plaça Barceloneta with Baroque church of San Miquel del Port
- Original houses on Calle Sant Carles
- Market on Plaça Font
- Passeig Marítim
- Plaça Brugada

INFORMATION

- ✚ H/J10; locator map F3
- ✉ Barceloneta
- 🚇 Barceloneta
- 🚌 17, 39, 45, 57, 64, 157
- ↔ Port Vell (▶ 46), Port Olímpic (▶ 50), Parc de la Ciutadella (▶ 48)
- ❓ Barceloneta's *Festa Major*, with music, parades, dancing on the beach, and fireworks runs through the 3rd week in September.

Port Olímpic and the Beaches

The eye-catching development of the Víla Olímpic, built for the 1992 Olympic Games, is a stunning ensemble of marinas, broad promenades, glittering buildings, and open space.

Port Olímpic The marina is the heart of the new Olympic district, built as the centrepiece of the water events, and backed by the apartments which once housed the athletes, leisure facilities, shops, seafront parks, and towering skyscrapers. Sleek and expensive yachts and boats of all shapes and sizes line the pontoons, and this is the place to come and hire a sailing boat if you want to take to the water. The enclosed marina, and the neighbouring promenades, are lined with bars and restaurants of all descriptions, firm favourites year-round with crowds of all ages. Inland, the tallest buildings are the Mapfre towers and the opulent Hotel Arts, part of a development that had as big an impact on Barcelona as the 19th-century construction of the Eixample.

Fun in the sun To either side of Port Olímpic lie clean, sandy beaches, attracting both visitors and Barcelonans. The beaches stretch north from Barceloneta to the new marine park at Diagonal Mar with its Thalassa bathing pools and yacht harbour. Spruced up in the late 1980s, the 8-km long esplanade is backed by tree-lined grassy spaces, offering cyclists, roller-bladers, and strollers an escape from the city. Along with watersports and beach games you'll find fresh-water showers, sunbed hire, children's play-parks and everything else you need for a day at the beach. And when the sun sets there are innumerable *chiringuitos* (beach bars) and restaurants in the Port Olímpic to refresh and revive.

Outdoor café in the shadow of Port Olímpic

BARCELONA's
best

51

Galleries & Museums

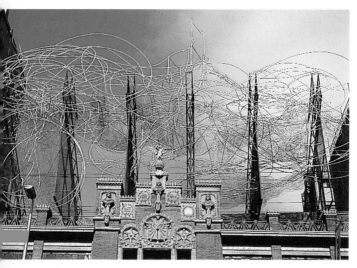

Cloud and Chair *at Fundació Antoni Tàpies*

THE *ICTÍNEO I*

This venerable ancestor of the Science Museum's submarine *Barcelona* can be seen at the waterfront in the Port Vell. Designed by the Catalan patriot and socialist inventor Narcis Monturio, the fish-shaped vessel was built in Barcelona's Nuevo Vulcano shipyard and launched in 1859. It proved supremely seaworthy despite the fact that it was driven solely by human muscle-power. Government indifference kept Spain from exploiting this surprising lead in submarine navigation.

CASA ASIA

An armchair traveller's journey into Central Asia and the Far East, this elegant museum brings together art, music, theatre, and cinema from Iran to Japan. The poster art and architecture exhibitions are well worth a look.

➕ H6 ✉ Palau Baró de Quadras, Diagonal 373 ☎ 93 238 7337 🕐 Tue–Sat 10–8; Sun 10–2 🍴 Café Ⓜ Diagonal 💲 Inexpensive

FUNDACIÓ ANTONI TÀPIES

Nowadays, Joan Miró's mantle as the Grand Old Man of Catalan art is convincingly worn by Tàpies, whose earthy creations can be seen in this magnificently converted *modernista* building by Domènech i Montaner. The building announces its purpose with Tàpies' roof-top sculpture *Cloud and Chair*, an extraordinary extrusion of wire and tubing.

➕ H7 ✉ Carrer d'Aragó 255, Eixample ☎ 93 487 03 15
🕐 Tue–Sun 11–8 🚇 Passeig de Gràcia ♿ Good
👜 Moderate

MUSEU DE LA CIENCIA I DE LA TÈCNICA

Housed in a splendid *modernista* building at the foot of the Tibidabo heights, this up-to-date Museum of Science and Technology is the finest of its kind in Spain. Many of its exhibits and displays encourage participation, and it is a great favourite with children, who have exclusive use of some of the facilities. There is an Optics Room, a Computer Room, a Planetarium, and a Foucault Pendulum. Perched outside is the museum's emblem, the submarine *Barcelona*.

www.noumuseudelaciencia.com ➕ G2 ✉ Teodor Roviralta 55 ☎ 93 212 60 50 🕐 Mon–Fri 9.30–8 🍴 Café 🚇 Tibidabo, then Tramvia Blau ♿ Good 👜 Moderate

MUSEU FREDERIC MARÈS

There are three main reasons for visiting this museum named after the long-lived sculptor and obsessive collector Frederic Marès: its setting overlooking the courtyard garden of the Royal Palace; its inexhaustible collection of sculpture from pre-Roman times to the 19th century; and last (but far from least), the section known as the Collecciò Sentimental (Sentimental Museum), with its surreal array of everyday objects from the 15th to the 19th centuries.

➕ H9 ✉ Plaça St. Iu 5 ☎ 93 310 58 00
🕐 Tue–Sat 10–7; Sun 10–3 🍴 Café 🚇 Jaume I
♿ Few 👜 Moderate. Free 1st Sun of month

MUSEU TÈXTIL I D'INDUMENTÀRIA

The very existence of the Museum of Textiles and Fashion is a reminder that Barcelona rode to prosperity in the 1800s on the back of the textile industry. The collection's range extends far beyond 19th-century Catalonia; there are costumes of all kinds, from the Middle Ages to more or less contemporary times—witness the inventive creations of Balenciaga. A bonus is the brace of medieval palaces housing the collection.

➕ H9 ✉ Montcada 12 ☎ 93 310 45 16
🕐 Tue–Sat 10–6; Sun 10–3 🍴 Café-restaurant
🚇 Jaume I ♿ Few 👜 Moderate

Exhibit from the Museu Frederic Marès

Modernista & Modern Architecture

CATALAN CREATION

The late 19th-century *modernista* movement embraced a contemporary interest in the decorative arts–buildings were ornamented with extraordinary detail, both inside and out. *Modernista* proponents believed that interior decoration and furniture were as important to a building as its facade. This "total art" concept infiltrated all areas of Barcelona; although the Eixample has a high concentration of *modernista* architecture, there are traces all across the city–in doorways, on paving patterns, railings, lamp posts, and even shop interiors.

The facade of the Casa Fuster

In the Top 25

- **9 CASA MILÀ (► 34)**
- **10 MANZANA DE LA DISCÒRDIA (► 35)**
- **15 PALAU DE LA MÚSICA CATALANA (► 40)**
- **4 PARC GÜELL (► 29)**
- **14 SAGRADA FAMILIA (► 39)**

CASA COMALAT

Many *modernista* architects gave their buildings an elaborate street facade, leaving the rear to look after itself. Salvador Valeri's Casa Comalat of 1911 is an exception, with gloriously over-the-top ornamentation on both frontages.

➕ H6 ✉ Diagonal 442/Corsega 316 🚇 Diagonal

CASA FUSTER

This corner building of 1910 on Passeig de Gràcia is one of Domènech i Montaner's last urban edifices, with a playful yet masterly combination of classical and neo-Gothic styles and motifs.

➕ H6 ✉ Gran de Gràcia 2–4/Passeig de Gràcia 132 🚇 Diagonal
🚌 22, 24, 28, 39

CASA MACAYA

Barcelona's medieval palaces served as models for Puig i Cadafalch's 1901 building, now a culture centre. It gives you a chance to explore the interior of one of the more sumptuous creations of Catalan *Modernisme*.

➕ J6 ✉ Centre Cultural de la Fundació La Caixa, Passeig de Sant Joan 108 ☎ 93 458 89 07 🕐 Tue–Sat 11–8; Sun and hols 11–3
🍴 Café 🚇 Verdaguer 💰 Inexpensive

CASA TERRADES

Puig i Cadafalch's huge 1905 building, known also as the Casa de les Punxes (House of Spikes), occupies the whole of an island site in the Eixample. Its profusion of towers and gables would seem to make it more at home in Bavaria than on the Mediterranean.

➕ H6 ✉ Diagonal 416–420 🚇 Diagonal

CASA VICENS

Gaudí's first major commission (1878), this summer residence in Gràcia is generally reckoned to have paved the way for *Modernisme*, less with its neo-Arabic decoration than with its structure and layout.

➕ H5 ✉ Carrer de les Carolines 18–24 🚇 Fontana 🚌 22, 24, 28, 39

HOSPITAL DE LA SANTA CREU I SANT PAU

Disliking the monotony of the Eixample, Domènech i Montaner deliberately defied it by aligning the buildings of Barcelona's first modern hospital at 45 degrees to its grid of streets. The hospital was laid

The striking edifice of the Hospital de Sant Pau

out like a self-contained village with patients housed in 48 separate pavilions; a profusion of decoration was intended to speed healing.

➕ K6 ✉ Sant Antoni Maria Claret 167 🚇 Hospital de Sant Pau

MIES VAN DER ROHE GERMANY PAVILION

Germany's contribution to the Expo of 1929 was this supremely cool construction of steel, glass, and marble that reinvented all the rules of architecture. It has become an icon of modern (as opposed to *modernista*) design. Yet amazingly, the building was demolished when the fair was over. It was rebuilt by devoted admirers in the mid-1980s and is now a compulsory stop for visiting international architecture students.

➕ E8 ✉ Pavelló Barcelona, Avinguda del Marquès de Comillas ☎ 93 423 40 16 🕙 Daily 10–8 🚇 Espanya 💳 Moderate

PALAU GÜELL

Gaudí's first mature work was this magnificent palace for his patron Eusebi Güell, begun in 1886. Painstakingly designed and constructed from the finest materials available at the time, it's a masterpiece. The paradoxical effect of simplicity and space amid all the innovation and finery is striking. The rooftop terrace, with chimneys decorated with glazed tiling, prefigures the work on the Casa Milà and is a particular delight.

➕ G9 ✉ Carrer Nou de la Rambla 3–5 ☎ 93 317 39 74 🕙 Mid-Mar to mid-Oct Mon–Sat 10–6.15, mid-Oct to mid-Mar Mon–Fri 10–4.30. Guideed tours only 🚇 Liceu

RELICS OF AN ERA

Modernista architecture was embraced by the Universal Exhibition of 1888 and was at its peak for the 20 years following the event. Many of the buildings from this time no longer exist, but Domènech i Montaner's exhibition restaurant, Castell dels Tres Dragons (Castle of the Three Dragons), has survived. This jolly neo-medieval brick and iron building was subsequently used by the architect as his studio and today houses the city's Zoological Museum.

55

Parks & Gardens

PROJECTS NOT PLANS

In the early 1980s, the City Council of Barcelona decided to encourage small-scale civic projects like parks and plazas rather than grandiose schemes. The results can be seen all over the city, where new paving, trees, and sculpture embellish the urban scene—and help to consolidate Barcelona's international reputation as a centre of exciting and progressive design.

JARDÍ BOTANIC

A fascinating insight into the flora that distinguishes Catalonia from Spain, and Spain from the rest of the world, this garden was planted in 1999 and is just starting to flourish. Its eight different zones showcase plants from Australia to the Balearic Islands.
➕ D8 ✉ C/Doctor Font i Quer 2 🕐 Nov–Mar, Mon–Sat 10–5; Apr–Oct, Mon–Fri 10–5, Sat and Sun 10–8 🚌 50, 51. Montjuïc at weekends 💰 Moderate. Guided tours available.

PARC DEL CLOT

This ingenious neighbourhood park in the eastern suburbs incorporates the walls of the old railway yards it replaced. Among the features are a plaza, overhead walkways, enigmatic sculptures, and artificial hills.
➕ L7 ✉ Escultors Claperós 🕐 May–Aug: daily 10–9. Apr–Sep: daily 10–8. Mar, Oct: daily 10–7. Nov–Feb: daily 10–6 🚇 Glories 💰 Free

PARC DE L'ESPANYA INDUSTRIAL

The postmodern design of Europe's oddest municipal park flies in the face of all the rules in the landscape architect's book. Trees are almost outnumbered by the giant lighthouses lined up along one side of the site; one plane tree grows out of a heap of rocks; and the Mediterranean sun beats down on the blinding white stairways. But children love the monster metal slide, styled to look like St. George and the Dragon, and there are always customers for the boats on the lake.
➕ E6/7 ✉ Cicero 🕐 Open access 🚇 Sants-Estació

PARC DEL FOSSAR DE LA PEDRERA

This new commemorative park was laid out in a quarry next to the splendid Cementiri del Sud Oest, which is notable for its extravagant *modernista* family tombs. Many of those on the losing side in the Civil War were buried here, including the president of Catalonia, Lluís Companys. His tomb is the modest, minimalist centrepiece of the park.
➕ C9 🚌 9, 38, 72, 109

PARC DEL LABERINT D'HORTA

Lovingly restored, this 18th-century retreat is on the wooded slopes of Vall d'Hebron high above the built-up area of Barcelona. One delight succeeds another as you explore steps and pathways leading from the neo-Arab mansion (once the focal point of the estate that was the basis for the park) to the

great pool at the top of the garden. There are fountains, canals, sculptures, and a gorge with a mock cemetery and hermit's hut. At the heart of the extensive garden is the eponymous Labyrinth, a beautiful maze with a statue of Eros at its centre.

➕ L1 ✉ Passeig dels Castanyers ⏲ May–Aug: daily 10–9. Mar, Apr, Sep, Oct: daily 10–8. Nov–Feb: daily 10–6 🚌 10, 27, 60, 73, 76, 85 ♿ None 💰 Inexpensive

PARC JOAN MIRÓ (PARC DE 'ESCARXADOR)

The sculptor's giant polychromatic *Woman and Bird* dominates this park with its orderly rows of palm trees. It is laid out on the site of an old slaughterhouse, l'Escorxador, where bulls were taken after fights at the nearby bullring.

➕ E7 ✉ Tarragona ⏲ Open access 🚇 Tarragona, Espanya

PLAÇA DELS PAÏSOS CATALANS

Basically a concrete canopy laid out on ground once occupied by railway tracks, this open space is more sculpture show than park: shining steel canopies take the place of trees.

➕ E6 ⏲ Open access 🚇 Sants-Estació

The rather bizarre and futuristic Parc de l'Espanya Industrial

TREES IN THE CITY

The natural vegetation of Barcelona is the evergreen oak. The noble plane trees that line so many streets, including the Rambla, were introduced into Spain some 600 years ago. New plantings favour the Italian cypress, a symbol of hospitality, and the date palm, brought back from the Spanish colonies a century or so ago.

Plaças

The very hub of cosmopolitan Barcelona —the Plaça de Catalunya

PLAÇA DE CATALUNYA IN THE CIVIL WAR

In the military uprising that signalled the start of the Civil War, the rebels' attempt to storm the telephone exchange on the eastern corner of the square was repelled by armed workers. Later, in the confused fighting between the rival parties of the Left, the Anarchists held the Raval district to the west, while the Communists commanded the square with a machine-gun mounted in the "O" of the rooftop sign of the old Hotel Colón.

PLAÇA DE CATALUNYA

City life seems to revolve around this spacious central square, not least because of its position at the upper end of the Rambla. The main landmark is the huge slab-like Corte Inglès department store; the population of monuments and statues is considerable and well worth a look. A 1991 addition commemorates the popular pre-Civil War politician Francesc Macià.

🛨 H8 🚇 Catalunya

PLAÇA DEL PÍ

Set amidst the warren of winding streets between the cathedral and the Ramblas you'll find Plaça del Pí and the adjoining Plaça Sant Josep Oriol, two of Barcelona's most beguiling squares. These asymmetrical spaces have leafy shade, laid-back cafés, and weekend art exhibitions, a great place to relax. Pí is named for the pines trees that once grew here, as is the serene church, Santa Maria del Pí (➤ 59).

🛨 G8 🚇 Liceu

PLAÇA REIAL

With its arcades and classical facades, this grandiose and splendidly symmetrical square is in complete contrast to the crooked streets and alleyways of the surrounding Barri Gòtic. Built in the mid-19th century on the model of the squares of Paris, it is a favourite hangout of idlers and winos, though it is considerably smarter than it once was. Antoni Gaudí designed the sinuous, wrought-iron lampposts, his first official commission by the city of Barcelona in the 1870s.

🛨 G9 🚇 Liceu

PLAÇA DEL SOL

This neat little square is a nice enough place for a coffee while wandering the streets of Gràcia by day, but it really comes into its own after dark, particularly at weekends. Café del Sol, with its cool *terraza* and El Dorado are well worth checking out before heading off to a club.

🛨 H5 🚇 Fontana

Churches

BETLEM

The Bethlehem Church, a landmark on the Rambla, was formed as a Jesuit foundation in 1681. As such, it aroused the particular fury of anti-clerical mobs in 1936, when its interior was torched and destroyed. The splendidly ornate porch remains.

✚ G8 ✉ Rambla 107/Carme 2 🚇 Liceu

DE LA MERCÉ

Together with St. Eulàlia, Our Lady of Mercy is one of Barcelona's patron saints. Her church, one of the finest baroque buildings in the city, was erected in the 1760s, replacing a much earlier building.

✚ H9 ✉ Plaça de la Mercé 🚇 Drassanes

SANTA MARIA DEL PÍ

The focal point of a trio of tiny squares, the monumentally plain exterior of this Barri Gòtic church conceals an equally austere interior, a single nave in characteristic Catalan Gothic style. The main façade, its statues long since gone, has a fine rose window. The octagonal bell tower is 180 feet high.

✚ G9 🕐 Weekdays 8.30–1, 4.30–9, otherwise 8–2, 5–9 🚇 Liceu

SANT MIQUEL DEL PORT

This fine mid-18th century baroque building faces the square named after it in the centre of Barceloneta.

✚ H10 ✉ Plaça de la Barceloneta 🚇 Barceloneta

SANT PAU DEL CAMP

It is a surprise to find a village church named St. Paul-in-the-Fields so close to the old city centre, but the Romanesque structure was in the middle of the countryside when it was built at the beginning of the 12th century. It replaced an older building, probably dating from Visigothic times, which was wrecked by Moorish invaders; some material from this original building was used to build the columns. The façade's simple and severe sculptural decoration includes the symbols of the Evangelists and the Hand of God.

✚ G9 ✉ Sant Pau 101 🕐 Mon, Wed–Sun 11–1, 6–7.30; Tue 11.30–12.30 🚇 Paral.lel

TRAGIC WEEK

The outbreak of the Civil War in 1936 saw the destruction of church interiors in Barcelona, but the Setmana Tragica (Tragic Week) of July 1909 was even worse; more than 80 religious buildings were burned and rioters danced in the streets with the disinterred bodies of priests and nuns.

Rose window inside Santa Maria del Pí

Sports & Amusements

Plaça d'Europa and Torre de Calatrare at the Olympic complex in Montjuïc

OUT OF TOWN

City dwellers though they may be, *Barcelonins* love the great outdoors. The Costa Daurada and Costa Brava are as popular with locals as they are with northern Europeans. Just behind the great city rises the Sierra de Collserola, with its forests and footpaths. The Pyrenees, two hours' drive away, have long been the preserve of Catalan climbing clubs.

In the Top 25

⑤ ANELLA OLÍMPICA (MONTJUÏC) (► 30)

ESTADI OLÍMPIC

The Barcelona Dragons play against other teams in the American Football World League on Sundays, April–June. Buy tickets on the day at the stadium.

🏠 E9 ✉ Avinguda de l'Estadi ☎ 93 425 49 49 🚌 61, 50

GALERIA OLÍMPICA

The video displays and souvenir showcases of this Olympic Gallery recall some of the glories of the Olympic fortnight in 1992.

🏠 E9 ✉ South Gate, Estadi Olímpic ☎ 93 426 60 60 🕐 Oct–Mar: Mon–Fri 10–1, 4–6; Sat, Sun 10–2. Apr–Jun: Mon–Sat 10–2, 4–7; Sun 10–2. Jul–Sep: Mon–Sat 10–2, 4–8; Sun 10–2 🚌 61, 50 👟 Inexpensive

NOU CAMP

The suppression of Catalan self-respect under the Franco regime made Barcelona soccer club (FC Barcelona) a potent symbol of identity. The passion "Barça" attracted then, particularly when pitted against rival Real Madrid, has not diminished despite today's more enlightened political climate. The 98,000-seat Nou Camp stadium is the home of the club and a great shrine of world soccer. If you want to go to a match, reserve early; most seats will be already taken by the club's 100,000-plus members. The museum under the terraces has an array of trophies and replays of magic moments.

Museo del Futbol Club Barcelona: 🏠 D5 ✉ Arístides Maillol ☎ 93 496 36 00 🕐 Mon–Sat 10–6.30; Sun and hols 10–2 🚇 Collblanc, Maria Cristina 🦽 Good 👟 Moderate

PARC D'ATRACCIONS DE TIBIDABO

Built on several levels of the mountain-top, high-tech attractions sit alongside traditional fairground rides—some features, like the red monoplane (1922) and the Haunted Castle (1955), have entertained for years.

🏠 G1 ✉ Plaça del Tibidabo ☎ 93 211 79 42 🕐 Mar–Apr: Fri–Sun noon–7. May: Thu–Sun noon–7. Jun: Wed–Sun noon–7. Jul–Aug: Mon–Thu, Sun noon–10; Fri, Sat noon–1AM. Sep: Mon–Thu noon–8; Fri–Sun noon–10. Oct: Sat, Sun noon–8 🚇 FGC Tibidabo then Tramvia Blau and funicular to park 👟 Expensive

VELODROM DE HORTA

Together with Montjuïc and the Olympic Village, the Vall d'Hebron on the lower slopes of the Sierra de Collserola was one of the three sites of the 1992 Olympics. The elliptical Velodrome was built to seat 14,000 for the 1984 World Cycling Championships.

🏠 L1 ✉ Passeig de la Vall d'Hebron 🚌 10, 27, 60, 73, 76

Attractions for Children

In the Top 25

21 AQUARIUM / IMAX CINEMA (PORT VELL)
(➤ 46)
6 POBLE ESPANYOL (➤ 31)

GOLONDRINES

Barcelona's swallow-boats (operating since 1888)
offer harbour trips from the Port Vell quayside.
Trips also go to Port Olímpic, poviding a different
perspective of the area.
www.lasgolondrinas.com ➕ G10 ☎ 93 442 31 06 ◑ Phone for
times ◪ Moderate

MUSEU DE CERA

The wax museum in the Rambla is an old favourite,
with exciting special effects. Look out for
Superman on the rooftop.
➕ G9 ✉ Passatge de la Banca, 7 ☎ 93 317 26 49 ◑ Jul–Sep:
daily 10–10. Oct–Jun: Mon–Fri 10–1.30, 4–7.30; weekends and hols
11–2, 4.30–8.30 ◪ Expensive

PARC DE LA CIUTADELLA

This large park (➤ 48), convenient to the city centre,
has playgrounds, bike and
skate rentals, and the Parc
Zoologic. A gorilla exhibition
commemorates Copito de
Nieve (Snowflake), who was
once the only albino gorilla
in captivity. In the separate
children's section, smaller
animals can be petted.
Zoo: ➕ J9 ☎ No phone ◑ Daily
10–sunset ◉ Barceloneta, Arc de
Triompf

MUSEU DE XOCOLATA

A museum devoted to
chocolate is bound to appeal
to children of all ages. Here
you'll find an overview of
the history of chocolate,
from its New World origins
to its arrival in Europe.
There are some staggering
chocolate creations,
including the elaborate
Easter *monos*, and a highly
tempting shop
➕ H9 ✉ Antic Convent de Sant
Agusti, Plaça Pons i Clerc ☎ 93 268
78 78 ◑ Mon, Wed–Sat 10–7; Sun
10–3 ◉ Jaume I ◪ Inexpensive

TRAVEL IN THE CITY

Discovering a new city always
delights children. Unusual
ways of travelling in Barcelona
include the vintage tram,
Tramvia Blau; the funicular up
to Tibidabo; and the funicular
and cable cars that serve
Montjuïc (➤ 30).

*The Rambla's street
entertainers*

61

What's Free

*Rambling along the
Carrer del Bisbe in the
Barri Gòtic*

WALKING THE STREETS

Even more than most cities,
the best way to experience
Barcelona, as well as the
cheapest, is on foot. Many
streets in the Barri Gòtic are
traffic-free, and the compact
nature of the old city means
that walking is often not only
the quickest way to get about,
but also the most interesting.

THE BEACH
Barcelona is one of those rare cities with a good
bathing beach. The sandy shore extends for more
than 2 miles from Barceloneta northward, with
children's playgrounds, plenty of showers, and good
access for people with disabilities.

MUSEUMS
Museums run by the City Council allow free entry on
the first Sunday of the month.

MUSEU DEL PERFUM
How appropriate that a scent museum should be
situated among the sleek shops and expensive
boutiques of the prestigious Passeig de Gràcia. The
5,000-item collection ranges from the time of the
Pharoahs to today.
➕ H7 ✉ Passeig de Gràcia 39 ☎ 93 216 01 46 🕐 Mon–Fri
10–2, 4–8; Sat 10–2. Closed hols 🚇 Passeig de Gràcia ♿ Few

PARKS
What a privilege to walk around Gaudí's Parc Güell
(➤ 29)—and it doesn't cost a euro. Alternatively,
explore the magnificent greenery embellishing the
slopes of Montjuïc or relax by the lake in the Parc de
la Ciutadella. Entry is free to all.

SARDANA
Circles of dancers perform the complex and carefully
controlled steps of Catalonia's national dance at a
number of places in the city, including the Cathedral
square. Be there at 6PM on Saturdays (Feb–Jul and
Sep–Nov only) or at noon on Sundays or holidays. Or
head for Plaça Sant Jaume (➤ 43) at 6PM on Sundays.
Turn up and dance or just watch if it all looks a little
complicated.

SCULPTURE
The City Council's vigorous promotion of new parks
and plazas included a project of public sculpture
(with the goal of creating focal points in otherwise
featureless suburban areas). This project has few
equals among modern cities, and you can come across
some startling modern sculpture in the most
surprising places. Prominent pieces include works by
Joan Miró (Parc Joan Miró ➤ 57), and Rebecca Horn
(Barceloneta/Port Olímpic ➤ 49–50).

STREET PERFORMERS
The entertainment along the Rambla is always free,
and the many human statues, jugglers, fire-eaters,
street musicians, and other talents can be surprisingly
good.

BARCELONA
where to...

Old City

CATALAN COOKING

Catalonia is generally reckoned to have one of the great regional cuisines of Spain. It is based on good ingredients from the varied countryside and on seafood from the Mediterranean and the Atlantic. Four principal sauces are used. There is *sofregit* (onion, tomato, and garlic cooked in olive oil); with added sweet pepper, aubergine, and courgette it becomes *samfaina*. *Picada* is made by pounding nuts, fried bread, parsley, saffron, and other ingredients in a mortar. Finally there is garlic mayonnaise, *alioli*.

AMAYA ($$)

Deservedly popular Basque restaurant and tapas bar specializing in seafood dishes.

✚ G9 ✉ Rambla 20–24 ☎ 93 302 10 37 🚇 Liceu, Drassanes

LA BELLA NAPOLI ($)

Hand-spun pizzas, a long list of anti-pasti, and a good selection of Italian wines are the order of the day at this casual Italian bistro. Drop in after a day exploring Montjuïc.

✚ F9 ✉ C/Margarit 14 ☎ 93 442 50 56 🚇 Tue–Sun 1.30–4PM, 8.30–midnight 🚇 Poble Sec

BIOCENTER ($)

The emphasis is on health and freshness at this busy vegetarian restaurant.

✚ G8 ✉ C/Pintor Fortuny 25, Raval ☎ 93 301 45 83 🚇 Lunch only. Closed Sun 🚇 Liceu

CAFÉ DE L'ACADEMIA ($$)

Not really a café at all, this restaurant offers some of the best deals in town on a variety of traditional Mediterranean cuisine.

✚ H9 ✉ Lledó 1, Ciutat Vella ☎ 93 315 00 26 🚇 Closed weekends and hols 🚇 Jaume I

CA L'ISIDRE ($$$)

The sophistication of the seasonal Catalan cooking has enticed King Juan Carlos to brave the distinctly unsophisticated surroundings to dine here when he is in Barcelona.

✚ F9 ✉ Les Flors 12, Poble Sec ☎ 93 441 11 39 🚇 Closed Sun and hols, also Sat Jun–Sep 🚇 Paral.lel (best by taxi)

CAN CULLERETES ($$)

Founded in 1786, Can Culleretes is one of the oldest restaurants in Barcelona. The menu is like a catalogue of old-fashioned Catalan cuisine, but there are modern dishes too. Sample the famous *botifarra* (pork sausage) with white beans.

✚ G9 ✉ Quintana 5, Ciutat Vella ☎ 93 317 64 85 🚇 Closed Sun evening, Mon, and Jul 🚇 Liceu

CASA LEOPOLDO ($$$)

Seafood and other fresh ingredients from the nearby Boqueria market have helped make the reputation of this excellent Catalan restaurant.

✚ G8 ✉ Sant Rafael 24, Raval ☎ 93 441 30 14 🚇 Closed Mon, hols and Sun PM 🚇 Liceu

COMERÇ 24 ($$$)

Charcoal grey walls streaked with red and yellow and a menu of all that's hot in the *tapas* world; chef Carles Abellán delights with creations such as "kinder egg surprise" (a soft boiled egg with truffle-infused yolk) and tuna sashimi pizza.

✚ J8 ✉ C/Comerç 24 ☎ 93 319 21 02 🚇 Tue–Fri 1.30–3.30PM, 8.30–midnight 🚇 Arc de Triomf

DRASSANES ($$)

Housed beneath the beautiful vaults of the Drassanes building, this is one of Barcelona's most imaginative restaurants, featuring superb Catalan cuisine.

✚ G9 ✉ Museu Marítim, Avda

Drassanes s/n, Raval ☎ 93 317 52 56 🕐 Closed PM Mon, Tue, Sun 🚇 Drassanes

LA FONDA ($)

Brisk, efficient service and great value Catalan cooking mean constant queues outside this three-floor restaurant.
➕ G9 ✉ Escudellers 10 ☎ 93 301 75 15 🕐 Closed Mon 🚇 Drassanes, Liceu

HAVANA VIEJA ($$)

Head here for the tastes and atmosphere of Cuba, with friendly crowds enjoying dishes where the accent is on piquant sauces and luscious puddings.
➕ H9 ✉ C/Banys Vells 2, La Ribera ☎ 93 268 25 04 🕐 Closed Sun PM 🚇 Jaume I

HOFMANN ($$$)

The inventive Mediterranean menu changes regularly and there's an extensive wine list. Friendly and efficient, Hofmann is one of the best restaurants in the old town.
➕ H9 ✉ Argenteria 74–78, Ciutat Vella ☎ 93 319 58 89 🕐 Closed Sat, Sun 🚇 Jaume I

LUPINO ($$)

Sleek designer lines and a chic cocktail bar help to make this El Raval's number one spot to see and be seen. Dishes are prepared with creative flair.
➕ G8 ✉ C/Carme 33 ☎ 93 412 36 97 🕐 Mon–Thu and Sun 1PM–4PM, 9PM–midnight, Fri and Sat 1PM–4PM, 9PM–1AM 🚇 Liceu

MESÓN DAVID ($)

In this robust Galician restaurant, portions are generous and the bustling character and friendly staff

add to the fun.
➕ G9 ✉ C/Carretas 63, Raval ☎ 93 441 59 34 🕐 Closed Wed and Aug 🚇 Paral.lel

MESÓN JESÚS ($)

Locals and foreigners flock to this cheap and cheerful restaurant to enjoy the Catalan and Spanish cooking served by the cheerful, busy staff.
➕ G9 ✉ C/Cecs de la Boqueria 4, Barri Gòtic ☎ 93 317 46 98 🕐 Closed Sat PM, Sun 🚇 Liceu

MOSQUITO ($)

The Asian inspired *tapas*, cheap wine and a chilled out atmosphere has made Mosquito a favourite with those looking for something a little different.
➕ H8 ✉ C/Carders 46 ☎ 93 268 75 69 🕐 Wed, Thu and Sun 7PM–1AM, Fri and Sat 7PM–2.30AM 🚇 Arc de Triomf

RESTAURANTE CASA REGINA ($$)

Country style décor and macrobiotic meals are on offer at this charming wholefood eatery. Choose from a lively salad bar, and free-range meats.
➕ H6 ✉ Riera de Sant Miguel 19 ☎ 93 237 86 01 🕐 Mon–Sat 1.30–4PM, Thu–Sat 9PM–11PM. Closed Sun and public holidays 🚇 Diagonal

SILENUS ($$)

The food at this relaxed restaurant is modern Mediterranean in style with the accent on quirky interpretations of traditional Catalan and Spanish dishes.
➕ G8 ✉ C/dels Angels 8, Rambla ☎ 93 302 26 80 🕐 Closed Sun 🚇 Liceu

GALICIAN FLAVOURS

Many restaurants in Barcelona specialize in Galician cuisine. Galicia, the northwest region of Spain, is famous for its seafood–octopus, crab, scallops, clams, and sardines are all simply prepared and delicious. Traditional Galician country fare is also excellent; try *empanadas* (pastry filled with seafood or meat).

Eixample & Gràcia

ALKIMIA ($$$)

The stark, minimal dining room can be a little sober, but it's the food that matters here. Chef Jordi Vila's brilliant cooking has won the hearts of Barcelona's foodies.

🔧 J6 ✉ C/Industria 79 ☎ 93 207 61 15 🕐 Mon–Sat 1.30–3.30PM, 9–11PM. Closed Sat lunch, Sun and public hols 🚇 Verdaguer, Hospital Sant Pau and Sagrada Família

L'ATZAVARA ($)

Be prepared to queue at this excellent vegetarian eating house, which offers imaginative salads, delicious soups, and good rice dishes.

🔧 G6 ✉ C/Muntaner 109, Eixample ☎ 93 454 59 25 🕐 Lunch only. Closed Sun and 3 weeks in Aug 🚇 Diagonal

BOTAFUMEIRO ($$$)

This spacious Galician restaurant on Gràcia's main street serves delicious shellfish and a selection of seafood from the country's Atlantic coast.

🔧 H6 ✉ Gran de Gràcia 81, Gràcia ☎ 93 218 42 30/93 217 96 42 🕐 Closed last 3 weeks Aug 🚇 Fontana

CA L'ABUELO ($)

The main draw at this superb-value restaurant is the help-yourself buffet, from where you can eat as much as you like from a huge range of salads, fish, seafood, meat, and desserts

🔧 H8 ✉ C/Providencia 44, Gràcia ☎ 93 284 44 94 🕐 Closed Sun, Mon; Tue, Wed, Thu PM 🚇 Fontana/Joanic

CASA CALVET ($$$)

This beautiful modern restaurant is housed in a Gaudí building and specializes in cutting edge Catalan cuisine. The service and ambiance are all you would expect in a top-class establishment.

🔧 H8 ✉ C/Casp 48, Eixample ☎ 93 412 40 12 🕐 Closed Sun 🚇 Urquinaona

CASI CASI ($$)

An Andalucian restaurant in the heart of Gràcia, serving delicious fresh fish and dishes such as *ajoblanco* (cold garlic soup).

🔧 G5 ✉ Laforja 8, esquina (corner) con C/Lincoln, Gràcia ☎ 93 415 8194 🕐 Closed Sun 🚇 Gràcia

CHIDO ONE ($)

Crammed full of Mexican kitsch and tequila bottles, the authentic Mexican dishes here include mammoth burritos, gusty mole sauces, mouth puckering ceviches and vats of fiery salsa.

🔧 H5 ✉ C/ Torrijos 30 ☎ 93 285 03 35 🕐 Mon–Fri 7PM–2AM, Sat and Sun 1PM–2AM 🚇 Diagonal, Passeig de Gràcia

EL GLOP ($)

Convenient to Gràcia, this trendy tavern serves delicious grilled meats.

🔧 J5 ✉ Sant Lluis 24, Gràcia ☎ 93 213 70 58/ 93 284 83 79 🚇 Joanic

JAUME DE PROVENÇA ($$$)

Interesting international dishes vary a menu of Catalan specialities, all prepared with refinement by acclaimed local chef Jaume Bargues.

🔧 F6 ✉ Provença 88, Sagrada Família ☎ 93 322 79

31 🕒 Closed Sun and Mon PM,
Aug, Christmas, and Easter
🚇 Encants

JEAN LUC
FIGUERAS ($$$)

This elegant restaurant at
the bottom end of Gràcia,
just off the Diagonal,
offers superb Catalan
cuisine—and the best
desserts in the city.
✚ H6 ✉ Santa Teresa 10,
Gràcia ☎ 93 415 28 77
🕒 Closed Sun 🚇 Diagonal

LAURAK ($$)

You'll find the best of
Basque cooking at this
splendid restaurant. Try
the gourmet menu to
experience the full range
of the kitchen's abilities.
✚ G6 ✉ C/La Granada del
Penedès 14–16, Gràcia ☎ 93
218 71 65 🕒 Closed Sun
🚇 FGC Gràcia

L'OLIVÉ ($$)

Good service and delicious
Catalan meat and seafood
dishes in a traditional
Eixample setting.
✚ G6 ✉ Balmes 47, Eixample
☎ 93 452 19 90 🕒 Closed
Sun evening 🚇 Paseo de
Gracia, Universitat

OROTAVA ($$$)

Although the art on the
walls vies with the food for
your attention, concentrate
on the carefully prepared
cocina de mercado, which
could include game as well
as succulent seafood.
Founded in the 1930s,
Orotava is one of the city's
favourite eating places.
✚ G7 ✉ Consell de Cent 335,
Gràcia ☎ 93 487 73 74/93
487 87 69 🕒 Closed Sun
🚇 Passeig de Gràcia

LE RELAIS DE VENISE

($$)

This meat lovers paradise
serves nothing but fat,
juicy steaks, perfect
pommes frites and a fresh
green salad. Fear not if the
portions look small, that's
only round one.
✚ H7 ✉ C/Pau Claris 142
☎ 93 467 21 62 🕒 Mon–Sat,
1.30–4PM, 8.30-12.30AM, closes
midnight Sun 🚇 Passeig de
Gràcia

RENO ($$$)

Exquisite Franco–Catalan
cuisine presented with
style. Reservations need to
be made in advance.
✚ G6 ✉ Tuset 27 ☎ 93 200
91 29 🕒 Closed Sat lunch and
Easter 🚇 Diagonal

TRAGALUZ ($$)

With 11 restaurants and
one hotel scattered across
town, you can't go wrong
with anything that falls
under the Tragaluz Group
umbrella. The original
shows off Barcelona's
definitive market cuisine
at its best.
✚ H6 ✉ Ptge. de la Concepció
5 ☎ 93 487 06 21
🕒 Mon–Wed 1.30–4PM,
8.30–midnight; Thu–Sat
1.30–4PM, 8.30–1AM
🚇 Diagonal, Passeig de Gràcia

WINDSOR ($$$)

French and Catalan
influences are found in
the sophisticated cuisine
of this lovely restaurant
with its pretty courtyard.
Seasonal menus, good
wine, and elegant decor
add to its attractions.
✚ H6 ✉ C/Còrsega 286,
Eixample ☎ 93 415 84 83
🕒 Closed Sat lunch and Sun
🚇 Diagonal

SPANISH MEATS

Although pork is the mainstay
of meat dishes, there is plenty
of choice for carnivores,
including brains, sweetbreads,
trotters, and other items that
have vanished from other
nations' tables. Beef and lamb
are good, and game is
excellent, including pheasant,
partridge, and wild boar (and
don't ignore the humble
rabbit). Try unusual
combinations like duck with
pears or meat with seafood.

Barceloneta & Port Olímpic

TIPS AND TAXES

There is no real fixed rate for tipping in restaurants. Some people leave a pile of whatever small coins they have in their pockets, others simply round up the total to the nearest euro. It is unusual to give more than a couple of euros even in the most sophisticated places. VAT is charged at 7 percent and is normally included in the total.

AGUA ($$$)

Watch the waves while you eat at this modern, laid-back restaurant, where dishes range from modern, innovative starters to traditional Catalan fare.
🔳 J10 ✉ Passeig Marítim de la Barceloneta 30, Port Olímpic ☎ 93 225 12 72 🕓 Open daily 🚇 Barceloneta

BESTIAL ($$)

Arguably the best seaside terrace in Barcelona, with wood decking and parasols, offering Italian fare at reasonable prices.
🔳 J10 ✉ C/Ramon Trias Fargas 2–4 ☎ 93 224 04 07 🕓 Mon–Thu 1.30–4PM, 8.30–midnight. Fri and Sat 1–5PM, 8.30–1AM, Sun 1–5PM, 8.30–midnight 🚇 Barceloneta

LA BOMBETA ($)

This no-frills cantina serves fresh fish and seafood, richly satisfying *bombas* (mashed potato balls stuffed with seasoned meat) and other classic *tapas* at excellent prices.
🔳 H10 ✉ C/de la Maquinista 3 ☎ No phone 🕓 Thu–Tue 10AM–midnight 🚇 Barceloneta

CAL PINXO ($$)

The latest restaurant from the famous Pinxo family of restaurateurs offers an excellent menu. Best of the restaurants housed in the converted Palau de Mar.
🔳 H9 ✉ Palau de Mar, Barceloneta ☎ 93 221 22 11 🚇 Barceloneta

EL CANGREJO LOCO ($$)

The crowds testify to the appeal of the reasonable prices on the *menú del día* of this large Port Olímpic seafood establishment.
🔳 K10 ✉ Moll de Gregal, Port Olímpic ☎ 93 221 17 48 🚇 Ciutadella

DZI ($$)

For a change of flavours try the classic pan-Asian cooking here, where old favourites are cooked with modern flair.
🔳 H10 ✉ Passeig de Joan de Borbó 76, Barceloneta ☎ 93 221 21 82 🕓 Open daily 🚇 Barceloneta

EL PASSADIS D'EN PEP ($$$)

There's no menu in this simplest of restaurants—just superb seafood, the best and freshest each day.
🔳 H9 ✉ Plaça del Palau 2, La Ribera ☎ 93 310 10 21 🕓 Closed Sun, hols and 3 weeks Aug 🚇 Barceloneta

SET PORTES ($$$)

Founded in 1836, the "Seven Doors" is one of Barcelona's most famous and reliable restaurants, serving up superb paella, fish, and seafood. You can book for the 1.30–2.30 and the 8–9.30 slots; otherwise be prepared to queue.
🔳 H9 ✉ Paseo de Isabell II 14, Port Vell ☎ 93 319 30 33 🕓 Open daily 🚇 Barceloneta

XIRINGUITÓ ESCRIBA ($$$)

Enjoy wonderful paellas, seafood, and the freshest of fish right on the seafront—leave a space for the wickedest desserts in town.
🔳 H10 ✉ Litoral Mar 42, Vila Olímpica ☎ 93 221 07 29 🕓 Closed Mon; Tue–Thu PM. Open daily for luch and dinner Jun–Sep 🚇 Ciutadella–Vila Olimpica

Upper Barcelona

ASADOR DE ARANDA ($$$)

The distinctive traditional roasts of Castile are served in the handsome setting of a *modernista* villa on the heights above the city. Sister branch Asador de Aranda II at Carrer Londres 94 is more centrally located in the Eixample, although not quite so grand.

✚ H3 ✉ Avinguda del Tibidabo 31 ☎ 93 417 01 15 🕐 Closed Sun evening 🚇 Tibidabo

LA BALSA ($$$)

Impeccable Catalan specialities are served here in a stylish setting just below the Tibidabo heights. The terrace offers stunning city views.

✚ G3 ✉ Infanta Isabel 4 ☎ 93 211 50 48 🕐 Closed Sun, and Mon lunch 🚇 Tibidabo

CAN TRAVI NOU ($$$)

There's a real country feeling in this restaurant situated in a lovely farmhouse set on a hill above the old village of Horta. Enjoy the splendidly traditional Catalan food in a timbered dining room or, weather permitting, outside in the garden. The wine list extends to 500 wines and *cavas*.

✚ K2 ✉ C/Jorge Manrique, Horta ☎ 93 428 03 01 🕐 Closed Sun eve 🚇 Horta

GAIG ($$$)

Carles Gaig's eponymous restaurant, family-run since 1869, is arguably the finest in Barcelona, serving outstanding traditional Catalan dishes with a twist. The pheasant in malt whisky sauce is exquisite.

✚ L5 ✉ Pl Maragall 402 ☎ 93 429 10 17 🕐 Closed Sun, Mon and hols 🚇 Horta

NEICHEL ($$$)

Alsatian chef Louis Neichel gives seasonal Catalan cuisine more than a touch of French *savoir-faire* at this stylish restaurant. The *menu degustación* is excellent.

✚ E4 ✉ Beltrán i Rózpide 1, Pedralbes ☎ 93 203 84 08 🕐 Closed Sun, Mon, Aug and hols 🚇 Palau Reial

L'ORANGERIE ($$$)

It's not cheap but then again, how often do you get to dine on top of the world? The scented gardens, a cliff-top swimming pool, attentive service and a world-class restaurant and wine cellar make this one of the city's most romantic venues.

✚ G1 ✉ Hotel Gran La Florida, C/de Vallvidrera al Tibidabo 83–93 ☎ 93 259 30 00 🕐 Mon–Sat 1–3.30PM, Sun 1–4PM for brunch, Sun–Wed 8.30–11PM, Thu–Sat 8.30–11.30PM 🚍 Best reached by taxi

VIA VENETO ($$$)

This innovative restaurant is attentive to every detail, and the Catalan fare is as refined as the setting is elegant. The location, in a smart part of town, attracts a clientele to match. The exclusive wine cellar and the creations of the pastry chef are outstanding.

✚ F5 ✉ Ganduxer 10–12, Les Corts ☎ 93 200 70 24 🕐 Closed Sat lunch and Sun 🚍 63 from Plaça Universitat

FISH FOR ALL

The seafood restaurants of Barcelona, concentrated in harbourside Barceloneta, are famous. They serve *zarsuela* (a seafood stew) and *suquet de peix* (fish and potato soup), as well as *fideus* (a paella-style dish with noodles instead of rice). *Arròs negre* is rice cooked in the black ink of a squid.

Tapas Bars & Cafés

P AND T

Pa amb tomàquet never fails to comfort a homesick Catalan and no meal is really complete without it. The local version of bread and butter, it consists of a slab of toasted *pa de pagès* (peasant bread) rubbed with a ripe tomato then drizzled with olive oil and spiked with a touch of garlic.

BAR DEL PÍ

Friendly service at this *tapas* bar delightfully located in the little square dominated by the church of Santa Maria del Pí.
➕ G/H9 ✉ Place Sant Josep Oriol 🚇 Liceu

BODEGA SEPÚLVEDA

The excellent value *menú del día* usually includes a good seafood dish. Or make a tasty meal of the varied *tapas*.
➕ G8 ✉ Sepúlveda 173bis ☎ 93 454 70 94 🕐 Closed Sun 🚇 Urgell

CAFÉ DE L'OPERA

Opera-goers and tourists fill the art nouveau interior and terrace tables of this dignified establishment opposite the Liceu. A great place for a spot of people-watching on the Rambla.
➕ G9 ✉ Rambla 74 ☎ 93 317 75 85 🚇 Liceu

LA ESTRELLA DEL PLATA

Revamped for the 90s, this old bar is now renowned for its superb and imaginative *tapas*, reckoned to be among the best in the city. Not cheap, but you get what you pay for.
➕ H9 ✉ Plaça del Palau ☎ 93 319 60 07 🕐 Closed Sun, and Mon lunch 🚇 Barceloneta

GINGER

Ginger is a place where the deep, leather arm chairs are just a bit too squidgy, the lights a bit too low, and the cocktails a bit too long and strong, to ever dream of leaving.
➕ H9 ✉ C/ Palma de Sant Just 1 ☎ 93 310 53 09 🕐 Tue–Thu 7PM–2.30AM, Fri and Sat 7–3AM 🚇 Jaume 1

HIVERNACLE

The elegant surroundings of the 19th-century glasshouse at the Parc de la Ciutadella are a relaxing place to stop for coffee.
➕ J9 ✉ Parc de la Ciutadella ☎ 93 268 01 77 🚇 Arc de Triomf

MAM I TECA

Somewhat off the beaten track, but well worth the effort of finding it for its cozy decor and superlative *charcuterie* and cheeses, served with a selection of the country's finest and most unusual wines.
➕ G8 ✉ C/Lluna 4 ☎ 93 441 33 35 🕐 Mon, Wed–Fri 7.30PM–1AM, Sat and Sun 1.30PM–1AM 🚇 Sant Antoni

MIRABLAU

There are superb city views from the terrace at this popular bar high on the slopes of Tibidabo, while the huge windows ensure that you can see equally well from inside.
➕ G1 ✉ Plaça Doctor Andreu ☎ 93 418 58 79 🕐 Open daily 🚇 FGC Tibidabo, then Tramvia Blau

PANS & COMPANY

A useful Catalan answer to fast food, with an emphasis on tomato and bread *pa amb tomàquet* (▶ 70). Various locations around the city.
➕ G8 ✉ Rambla 123 ☎ 93 301 66 21 🚇 Liceu

ELS QUATRE GATS

No visit to Barcelona is complete without a pause

at this shrine of *Modern-isme*. The Four Cats was frequented by Barcelona's turn-of-the-century bohemian crowd (including Picasso), two of whom are depicted in the famous picture (a reproduction) of arty types riding a tandem bicycle. Bar up front and a restaurant in the back.
🏠 H8 ✉ Montsio 3bis ☎ 93 302 41 40 🕐 Daily 🚇 Urquinaona, Catalunya

QUIMAT & QUIMET
More a *bodega* than a bar, this incredibly popular joint has a great selection of wine behind the bar and a good range of *tapas*.
🏠 F9 ✉ Poeta Cabañas 25 ☎ 93 442 31 42 🕐 Closed Aug 🚇 Paral·lel

SALAMBÓ
A friendly café, with a youngish clientele, this elegant Gràcia bar has an evocative 1930s feel and plenty of tables—excellent for sandwiches and salads. Wide range of drinks of all types, particularly brandies and whiskies.
🏠 H5 ✉ Torrijos 51 ☎ 93 218 69 66 🕐 Open daily 🚇 Joanic

SCHILLING
This popular café bar, between the Rambla and the Plaça St. Jaume, does great hot chocolate and sandwiches, and scoops a range of ice creams.
🏠 H9 ✉ Ferran 23 ☎ 93 317 67 87 🚇 Liceu

TALLER DE TAPAS
With its buff stone walls and historically placed terraces this *"tapas workshop"* offers classic

Spanish *tapas*, all freshly made to order; try grilled baby clams and giant Palamos prawns, velvety pan-fried duck's liver, and veal entrecots in bite-sized portions.
🏠 G9 ✉ Pl. Sant Josep Oriol 9 ☎ 93 301 80 20 🚇 Liceu ✉ C/ Argentería 51 ☎ 93 268 85 59 🚇 Jaume 1 🕐 Daily noon–midnight

TÈXTIL CAFÉ
A wonderful place to pause after the Picasso Museum, this elegant bar has tables set in the courtyard of the 14th-century palace that now houses the textile museum—good snacks and cooling drinks.
🏠 H9 ✉ Montcada 12–14 ☎ 93 268 25 98 🕐 Closed Mon 🚇 Jaume 1

VASO DEL ORO
Named after the beer, or, "cup of gold," that is brewed in-house, this long, pencil-thin bar serves wonderful *tapas*, but get in early if you want a seat.
🏠 J10 ✉ C/ Balboa 7 ☎ 93 319 30 98 🕐 Daily 9–midnight 🚇 Barceloneta

LA VINYA DEL SENYOR
This *petit bodega* has one of the best wine selections in town, most of which are available by the glass. There's more space in the summer, when tables spill onto the terrace overlooking the Santa Maria del Mar church.
🏠 H9 ✉ Plaça Santa Maria 5 ☎ 93 310 33 79 🕐 Tue–Thu, Sun noon–1AM, Fri and Sat noon–2AM. Closed Mon 🚇 Jaume 1

DIFFERENT DRINKS
Barcelona tapwater is drinkable, but not particularly appetizing. Most people are prepared to pay that little extra for mineral water *amb gas* (with bubbles) or *sens gas* (still). A soft drink unique to Spain is *horchata* (orxata in Catalan), a milk-like drink extruded from the crushed nut called a *chufa*. It takes a little getting used to but is deliciously refreshing once you have acquired the taste.

Malls & Department Stores

MORE THAN A MALL

Spain seems to have caught on to Anglo-Saxon ideas of supermarkets and shopping malls relatively late. First to arrive in Barcelona were the elegant Eixample malls specializing in fashion. Now there are monster malls like Glòries, plugged into the suburban expressway network. Though the malls are interesting enough in themselves, shopping is far more of a holiday experience in the galleries and boutiques of the Eixample or tucked away throughout the city.

EL CORTE INGLÉS

Synonymous in Spain with the concept of the department store, the Corte Inglés has no competition in Barcelona; virtually everything you could ever need is here under the roof of an aircraft-carrier-like establishment on Plaça de Catalunya. On the several floors between the splendid supermarket in the basement and the eagle's-nest eating place at the top are designer fashions, cosmetics, jewellery, a hairdressers, handicrafts, a stationery shop, a bookshop, a travel bureau, and an interpreter service.
H8 Plaça de Catalunya 14 93 306 38 00 Catalunya

MALLS

BULEVARD ROSA

The prototype of Barcelona's fashion malls, the Bulevard Rosa boasts 100-plus boutiques with the best in fashion, shoes, and accessories.
H7 Passeig de Gràcia 53–5 (also at Diagonal 474) 93 309 06 50 Passeig de Gràcia

LES GLÒRIES

More than 200 shops at the eastern end of the Diagonal, including international names, and an excellent supermarket, Carrefour.
K7 Diagonal 208 93 486 04 04 Glòries

MAREMAGNUM

Best approached via the Rambla del Mar and the southwest entrance with a spectacular mirror canopy, Maremagnum, in the middle of the Old Port, contains not only fashion boutiques, but also gift shops, cafés, restaurants, bars, and nightspots.
G10/11 Moll d'Espanya 93 225 81 00 Drassanes

EL TRIANGLE

New complex on the Plaça Catalunya, containing—among other shops—FNAC and Habitat. FNAC is one of the city's best sources for books, with a large English section, videos, and compact discs. The huge perfume and cosmetics shop, Sephora, takes up the whole basement floor and is invariably crowded, and there is also a branch of the popular men's fashion chain Massimo Dutti. The complex has an inexpensive café with a *terraza*.
H8 Plaça Catalunya 4 93 318 01 08 Catalunya

LATE OPENING

OPEN COR

Barcelona's newest late-night shops are run by El Corte Inglés and offer everything for insomniacs from food and drink to flowers and magazines.
H8 Ronda de Sant Pere 33 93 342 73 02 Urquinaona

VIP'S

Another late-night opener with a whole range of goods including books. There is a restaurant, too.
H8 Rambla de Catalunya 7–9 93 317 48 05 Catalunya

Arts, Crafts & Design

ASPECTOS

A Barcelona household furnishings design shop, with the work of established designers as well as the young and up-and-coming.

H9 ✉ Rec 28 ☎ 93 319 52 85 Ⓜ Jaume I

B D EDICIONES DE DISEÑO

A virtual museum of modern furniture design from the likes of Charles Rennie Mackintosh and Antoni Gaudí to the more contemporary Ricardo Bofill, in a building by Doménech i Montaner.

H7 ✉ Mallorca 291 ☎ 93 458 69 09 Ⓜ Passeig de Gràcia

CENTRE CATALÀ D'ARTESANIA

Established in 1985, the centre aims to promote Catalan crafts of every description—textiles, ceramics, metalwork, and traditional basketwork.

H7 ✉ Passeig de Gràcia 55 ☎ 93 467 46 60 Ⓜ Passeig de Gràcia

DOM

This eccentric and highly affordable emporium stocks treasures from the 60s and 70s including reproduction lava lamps, inflatable chairs, and printed shower curtains.

H9 ✉ C/Avinyó 7 ☎ 93 342 55 91 Ⓜ Jaume I

DOS I UNA

An early proponent of contemporary design, this establishment is filled with superior gift items.

H6 ✉ Rosselló 275 ☎ 93 217 70 32 Ⓜ Diagonal

GOTHAM

Restored furniture and an eclectic selection of lamps from the 1950s, 60s, and 70s, as well as many art deco pieces.

G9 ✉ Cervantes 7 ☎ 93 412 46 47 Ⓜ Jaume I

ICI ET LÀ

Fabulously quirky, this furniture and interior design shop stocks the creations of 40 or so different artists.

H9 ✉ Plaça Santa Maria del Mar 2 ☎ 93 268 11 67 Ⓜ Jaume I

LA MANUAL ALPARGATERA

All kinds of woven items, some created before your eyes. The speciality: hand-made espadrilles.

H9 ✉ Avinyó 7 ☎ 93 301 01 72 Ⓜ Liceu

NEOCERÀMICA

Spanish and international ceramic floor and wall tiles.

G3 ✉ Mandri 43 ☎ 93 211 89 58 Ⓜ La Bonanova 🚌 14 from Plaça de Catalunya

PILMA

Something of a Barcelona institution, this pillar emporium of designer goods for the home stocks everything from cactus shaped floor lamps to sleek Phillipe Stark furniture and kitchenware. www.pilma.com

G5 ✉ Diagonal 403 ☎ 93 416 1469 Ⓜ Diagonal

SALA PARÉS

The city's best art gallery, showing works of leading Catalan artists.

G8 ✉ C/Pretritxol 5 ☎ 93 318 70 20 Ⓜ Liceu

WHAT TO BUY IN THE BARRI GÒTIC

The intricate streets and alleyways of the old town east of the Rambla are full of individual shops selling virtually everything you might want to either eat or admire. There are craftsman's candles, cured hams, and all kinds of antiques and art objects. Portaferrissa and Portal de l'Angel streets have fashion boutiques and shoe shops.

Fashion

ELEGANT SHOPPING IN THE EIXAMPLE

For many visitors, Barcelona's main attraction is its stylish fashion shops. The most prestigious shopping area is in the Eixample, in the area between Gran Vía de les Corts Catalanes, Carrer de Balmes, Passeig de Gràcia, and Avinguda Diagonal. If you can't afford what's on offer, window shopping is an experience to be savoured, not only for the quality and sophisticated display of the goods but also for the many *modernista* buildings in the area.

ADOLFO DOMÍNGUEZ

Spain's brightest fashion star, renowned for linen suits, designed the shop as well as the super-stylish (and pricey) clothes.
✚ H7 ✉ Passeig de Gràcia 89 (and at three other locations in the city centre) ☎ 93 215 13 39 🚇 Passeig de Gràcia

ANTONIO MIRÓ

One of Spain's top designers, Miró is best known for his men's fashions, but he also has a range of women's and children's clothes, shoes, eyeglasses, and furniture.
✚ H7 ✉ Carrer Consell de Cent 349–351 ☎ 93 487 06 70 🚇 Passeig de Gràcia

ARMAND BASI

Basi is one of Spain's favourite designers and you'll find his full range for both men and women at this flagship store—everything from suits and knitwear to evening clothes and accessories.
✚ H7 ✉ Passeig de Gràcia 49 ☎ 93 215 14 21 🚇 Passeig de Gràcia

LE BOUDOIR

This heaven-sent lingerie shop stocks lacy corsetry and gorgeous silk and lace underwear.
✚ H8 ✉ C Canuda ☎ 93 302 52 81 🚇 Catalunya

CACHE CACHE

Natty togs for toddlers and older children.
✚ H7 ✉ Valencia 282 ☎ 93 215 40 07 🚇 Passeig de Gràcia

CANDELA

From fun and funky to supremely wearable, dress to impress in groovy outfits by hip local designers.
✚ H9 ✉ C/Santa Maria 6 ☎ 93 319 91 87 🚇 Jaume 1

CATIMINI

Attractive children's clothes shop. Displays are all colour-coordinated to help you match outfits.
✚ H6 ✉ Passeig de Gràcia 100 ☎ 93 215 77 94 🚇 Diagonal

CONTRIBUCIONES Y MODA

Step into high fashion (albeit last year's models, but who'll notice?) at a bargain price.
✚ H6 ✉ Riera de Sant Miquel 30 ☎ 93 218 71 40 🚇 Diagonal

CUSTO

Europe's most sought-after label for loud, figure-hugging T-shirts that are pieced together out of mismatched fabrics and emblazoned with brilliant images and icons.
✚ H9 ✉ C/Ferran 36 ☎ 93 342 66 98 ✉ Plaça de les Olles 7 ☎ 93 268 78 93 🚇 Jaume 1

DAVID VALLS

Original knitwear with eye-catching colours, styles, and textures.
✚ H7 ✉ Valencia 235 ☎ 93 487 12 85 🚇 Passeig de Gràcia

GONZALO COMELLA

After dressing three generations of Barcelona's affluent, this institution is changing with the times and you'll find far more designer labels.
✚ H7 ✉ Passeig de Gràcia 6 ☎ 93 412 66 00 🚇 Passeig de Gràcia

GROC

Tempting creations for both men and women by Catalonia's favourite designer, Toni Miró.

✚ H6 ✉ Rambla de Catalunya 100bis (also – women's wear only – at Muntaner 385) ☎ 93 215 01 80 Ⓜ Diagonal

HITA

This beautiful lingerie shop has exquisite nightwear, underwear, and bathroom accessories, beautifully made in silk, satin, purest cotton, and handmade lace.

✚ H7 ✉ Rambla de Cataluña 82 ☎ 93 215 19 27 Ⓜ Passeig de Gràcia

JEAN-PIERRE BUA

Barcelona's most chic (and wealthy) line up here each season for creations as startling as the decor.

✚ G5 ✉ Diagonal 469 ☎ 93 439 71 00 🚌 7, Tombus

JOSEP FONT

Beloved by women for his feminine lines, innovative, stand-alone design, and extraordinary eye for fabrics, Font is one of the leading exponents of Catalan fashion.

✚ H6 ✉ C/Provença 304 ☎ 93 300 31 11 Ⓜ Passeig de Gràcia

MANGO

International chain of women's fashion stores with attractive, well-made clothes in good fabrics at affordable prices. There are several branches throughout the city.

✚ H7 ✉ Passeig de Gràcia 65 ☎ 93 215 75 30 Ⓜ Passeig de Gràcia

MASSIMO DUTTI

Natty designs at more than reasonable prices in this nationwide outlet. Shirts are a speciality here.

✚ G6 ✉ Via Augusta 33 ☎ 93 217 73 06 Ⓜ Diagonal

MILANO

Stylish men's suits, jackets, and overcoats at bargain prices. Very popular.

✚ G8 ✉ La Rambla 138 ☎ 93 317 47 12 Ⓜ Drassanes

RIERA BAIXA SECOND-HAND MARKET

A pretty, pedestrianized street filled with retro boutiques, flea market stores, costume houses and other knick-knack emporiums. Check it out on a Saturday afternoon when the stores spill on to the pavement and vintage bargains abound.

✚ G8 ✉ C/Riera Baixa ☎ No phone Ⓜ Sant Antoni

STOCKLAND

The place for end-of-line designer fashions at attractive prices.

✚ H8 ✉ C/Comtal 22 ☎ 93 318 03 31 Ⓜ Urquinaona

ZARA

This mass operation is now a national and international success story, with branches all over Europe. The designs are up-to-the-minute and well priced. The attractive three-floor shop near Place Catalunya should be your first stop if you want a bargain, but there are branches city-wide.

✚ G8 ✉ C/Pelai 58 ☎ 93 301 09 68 Ⓜ Catalunya

DESIRABLES OF THE DIAGONAL

A zone of fine shops extends along the great avenue known as the Diagonal between Plaça Joan Carles I and Plaça Francesc Macià. Just off the avenue is one of the city's most fashionable shopping streets, Avinguda Pau Casals; in these shops and adjacent shopping centres, those who would like to consider themselves a cut above the common herd on downtown Rambla, can be seen.

Shoes & Accessories

FINE DESIGN

Barcelona's design tradition and its endless array of unusual and individual shops make the hunt for gifts and accessories unusally enjoyable. Fine leather goods at reasonable prices are to be found everywhere in the Eixample, and there are numerous expensive jewellery shops. In the Old Town, look for hand-painted jewellery, porcelain, and wooden crafts.

AGATHA

The French designer, sells inexpensive jewellery that ranges from classic designs to decidedly off-beat.
➕ H7 ✉ Rambla de Cataluña 112 ☎ 93 415 59 98 Ⓜ Passeig de Gràcia

CAMPER

Male and female, everyone in Barcelona seems to have a pair of Camper's well-made, comfortable, and stylish shoes. You can buy them in a handful of shops around the city and in department stores, including El Corte Ingles.
➕ H7 ✉ Valencia 249 (also at Pau Casals 5 and Muntaner 248) ☎ 93 215 63 90 Ⓜ Passeig de Gràcia

CASAS

Fashionistas adore Casa's monumental range of the season's must-haves; from spike-heeled stilettos to intricately patterned brogues both made in Spain and from abroad.
➕ H8 ✉ Portal de l'Angel 40 ☎ 93 302 11 12 Ⓜ Catalunya

GLAMOOR

Don't forget your prescription, because you'll find lenses and frames are much cheaper here than in Britain. The funkiest frames and the hippest labels in town.
➕ H9 ✉ C/Calders 10 ☎ 93 310 39 92 Ⓜ Jaume I, Barceloneta

GUIA GLOBAL

Wacky animal print cowboy hats and other striking headgear.
➕ G8 ✉ C/Tallers 1 ☎ 93 318 43 40 Ⓜ Catalunya, Universitat

HIPÒTESIS

Outstanding modern jewellery by Spanish and international designers.
➕ H6 ✉ Rambla de Cataluña 105 ☎ 93 215 02 98 Ⓜ Provença

LOEWE

World-renowned specialists in skins, Loewe's is known for its leather clothes, handbags, wallets, and suitcases. The shop occupies one of the finest buildings on Passeig de Gràcia: Domènech i Montaner's Casa Lleo Morera.
➕ H7 ✉ Passeig de Gràcia 35 (also at Diagonal 570, Plaça Pio XII, and Juan Sebastian Bach 8) ☎ 93 216 04 00 Ⓜ Passeig de Gràcia

ROYALTY

Huge selection of footwear by all the top names as well as the shop's own designers. There's a new collection each season.
➕ H8 ✉ Avenguida del Portal de l'Angel 38 ☎ 93 317 16 32 Ⓜ Metro Catalunya

SOLÉ

On an appropriately named street, this shop specializes in footwear in larger sizes.
➕ G9 ✉ Ample 7 ☎ 93 301 69 84 Ⓜ Drassanes

SPLEEN

Here you'll find over-the-top wacky costume jewellery, old fashioned hat pins, outlandish brooches, diamante tiaras, silk scarves, felt hats, and pearl-encrusted evening bags.
➕ H7 ✉ Passeig de Gràcia 55 ☎ 93 215 71 01 Ⓜ Passeig de Gràcia

Books & Music

ALTAÏR
A profusion of books
and maps on destinations
worldwide, including
Barcelona, Catalonia,
and Spain.
➕ H7 ✉ Avenida Gran Via
616 ☎ 93 342 7171
🚇 Passeig de Gràcia

BCN BOOKS
This bookshop offers a
good selection
of classics and modern
fiction from around the
world in English, along
with teaching materials
and foreign language
dictionaries. Well worth a
browse when you've run
out of reading material.
➕ H6 ✉ Provença 291
☎ 93 476 33 43
🚇 Diagonal

CASTELLÓ
A chain of music shops
with varying specialities:
Nou de la Rambla
concentrates on pop, folk,
and world music; Tallers 3
specializes in classical
music.
➕ G9 ✉ Nou de la Rambla 15
(and at Tallers 3) ☎ 93 302 42
36 🚇 Liceu

CRISOL
Books (including titles in
English), foreign-
language newspapers and
periodicals, CDs, and
videos on two floors.
Open until late.
➕ G7 ✉ Rambla de Cataluña
81 (and at Consell de Cent 341)
☎ 93 215 27 20 🚇 Passeig
de Gràcia

FNAC
A one-stop shop for
English language books,
international magazines,
all genres of music,

movies and computer hard
and software.
➕ H8 ✉ El Triangle, Plaça
Catalunya 4 ☎ 93 344 18 00
🚇 Catalunya

HAPPY BOOKS
A literary supermarket
with books piled high
—look out for some at
bargain prices. Well worth
a browse.
➕ G8 ✉ Pelai 20 (and at
Passeig de Gràcia 77) ☎ 93
317 07 68 🚇 Catalunya

LAIE
The ultimate literary
café, with a wonderful
selection of books
downstairs, including
travel maps and guides.
Atmospheric bar and
eaterie upstairs complete
with periodicals to peruse
while you relax.
➕ H7/8 ✉ Pau Claris 85
☎ 93 318 17 39 🚇 Passeig
de Gràcia

LIBRERIA HERDER
A superbly serious
bookstore with
impeccable academic
credentials. Strengths are
in languages and science
and there are many
international publications
(particularly in German).
➕ G7 ✉ Balmes 26 ☎ 93
317 05 78 🚇 Passeig de
Gràcia, Universitat

LLETRAFERIT
This New York style café-
cum-art gallery-cum-book
store by day, segues
effortlessly and somewhat
bizarrely, into a chic
cocktail bar by night. Well
woth a visit.
➕ G8 ✉ C/Joaquim Costa 43
☎ 93 301 19 61
🚇 Universitat, Sant Antoni

READING HABITS
There are plenty of bookshops
in Barcelona and many of
them stock publications in
foreign languages (especially
English). Newsstands are
crammed with magazines
dealing with every conceivable
subject, including the adult
comics that seem to fascinate
Spanish readers. Always
prominent is the
phenomenally successful
glossy *Hola!*, whose
preoccupation with the doings
of the rich and famous has
spawned imitators like the
British *Hello!*

Food Shops & Markets

PICNIC PLACES

Look out for the offerings from the *forn de pa* (bakery) and the *xarcuteria* (delicatessen or charcuterie). Don't miss slicings from a good *jamón serrano* (dry-cured ham). Look for *fuet* (a hard Catalan sausage), *chorizo, sabrasada* (a Mallorcan paste of pork and paprika), and cured *Manchego* cheese.

LA BOQUERIA

A city landmark, this superb market hall was built in the 19th century to house the food stands that cluttered up the Rambla and its surrounding streets. Beyond the market's gaping entrance arch are countless stands piled high with every foodstuff from the Mediterranean and its Catalonian hinterland. Amid the riot of colour and smells, marvel at a hundred species of fish, gorgeous vegetables, fragrant herbs, and animal parts that you may not have dreamed existed—all temptingly arranged.

➕ G8 ✉ Rambla 91 ☎ 93 318 25 84 Ⓜ Liceu

LA BOTIFARRERÍA DE SANTA MARÍA

A mouth-watering array of hand-made sausages ranging from wild boar and forest mushroom, to less conventional snail and sepia, and *vino ranci* and beetroot.

➕ H9 ✉ C/Santa Maria 4 ☎ 93 319 91 23 Ⓜ Jaume I

CASA DEL BACALAO

Dried salt cod features heavily in Catalan and Spanish cooking and this splendid shop sells nothing else—they'll vacuum pack a piece for you to take home.

➕ H8 ✉ C/Comtal 8 ☎ 93 301 65 39 Ⓜ Urqinaona

CASA GISPERT

Founded in the 1850s, this establishment is an expert roaster of nuts and coffees, and purveys everything from fresh-roasted hazelnuts and almonds to Iranian pistachios.

➕ H9 ✉ Sombrerers 23 ☎ 93 319 75 35 Ⓜ Jaume I

COCAO SAMPAKA

Sampaka's revolutionary chocolate making methods (olive, truffle or anchovy), hand-painted designs, and unique tasting room.

➕ H7 ✉ C/Consell de Cent 292 ☎ 93 272 08 33 Ⓜ Passeig de Gràcia

LA COLMENA

Cakes of all description, biscuits, and sweets in this traditional shop.

➕ H9 ✉ Plaça del Angel 12 ☎ 93 315 13 56 Ⓜ Jaume I

ESCRIBÀ PASTISSERIES

The city's most delicious creations in chocolate lie behind the *modernista* shopfront of the Antigua Casa Figueras.

➕ G8 ✉ Rambla 83 (also at Gran Via de les Corts Catalanes 546) ☎ 93 301 60 27 Ⓜ Liceu

FORMATGERIA LA SEU

This shop, dedicated to Spanish and Catalan cheeses, occupies the site of Barcelona's first butter-making factory. Pop in for a tasting with wine, before stocking up on hard-to-get treats for home.

➕ H9 ✉ C/ Dagueria 16 ☎ 93 412 65 48 Ⓜ Jaume I

VILA VINITECA

This friendly and helpful wine shop offers a superb selection of Catalan and Spanish wines, tastings and courses for those wanting to learn more.

➕ H9 ✉ C/ Agullers 7–9 ☎ 93 310 19 56 Ⓜ Jaume 1, Barceloneta

Gifts & Antiques

BARRI GÒTIC ANTIQUES MARKET

Bric-a-brac rather than heirloom bargains dominate the stands in front of the cathedral.

➕ H8 ✉ Avinguda de la Catedral 6 ☎ 93 291 61 18 🕐 Thu 9–8 🚇 Jaume I

BULEVARD DELS ANTIQUARIS

Every kind of antique dealer can be found in this complex of over 70 shops next to the Bulevard Rosa mall.

➕ H7 ✉ Passeig de Gràcia 55 ☎ 93 215 44 99 🚇 Passeig de Gràcia

CASA CONSISTORIAL/ ARTESANÍA MARCO

The Spanish Village, where this is located (► 31), may seem like a huge gift store but the huge array of hand-made ship models here is varied and reasonably priced.

➕ E8 ✉ Poble Espanyol ☎ 93 423 93 95 🚇 Espanya 🚌 13, 61

ELS ENCANTS FLEA MARKET

Patient searching can reveal gold among the dross of worn clothing, broken furniture, and other unwanted items. Plan your visit for around 8AM for the best selection.

➕ K7 ✉ Plaça de les Glòries ☎ 93 246 30 30 🕐 Mon, Wed, Fri, and Sat 8–7 🚇 Glòries

GERMANES GARCÍA

Baskets of every type spill out onto the pavement here, inside there's a huge array of wickerwork.

➕ H9 ✉ C/Banys Nous 15 ☎ 93 318 66 46 🚇 Liceu

GOTHAM

Since 1994, Gotham has been a favourite among Almódovar's set designers for its retro furniture from the 1930s through to the 70s. It is a paradise of kitsch and design classics.

➕ H9 ✉ C/Cervantes 7 ☎ 93 412 46 47 🚇 Jaume 1

MONTCADA TALLER

Above average crafts shop selling colourful Spanish ceramics, glassware, prints, and paintings. Perfect for unusual gifts to take home.

➕ H9 ✉ Placeta Montcada 10 bis ☎ 93 319 1581 🚇 Jaume 1

PLAÇA REIAL: COIN AND STAMP MARKET

The Plaça Reial plays host every Sunday to standholders and collector types indulging their enthusiasms.

➕ G9 ✉ Plaça Reial ☎ 93 291 61 18 🕐 Sun 9–2.30 🚇 Liceu

PLAÇA DE SANT JOSEP ORIOL: PICTURE MARKET

Barcelona's appealing counterpart to Paris's Montmartre art market takes place in one of the Barri Gòtic's most picturesque squares on Sundays. Worth a browse.

➕ G9 ✉ Plaça de Sant Josep Oriol ☎ 93 291 61 00 🕐 Sun 9–6 🚇 Liceu

SERVICIO ESTACIÓN

The biggest hardware store in Barcelona where you can choose from groovy paper bags to fruit-patterned lino and any number of other treasures.

➕ H7 ✉ C/Aragó 270 ☎ 93 216 02 12 🚇 Passeig de Gràcia

GOLDEN GIFTS

Among the touristy shops of the Spanish Village–the Poble Espanyol (► 31)–keep an eye peeled for gold: you can watch metalworkers and others actually producing some of the items for sale and there are outlets for unusual and original gifts and souvenirs.

Bars, Discos & Clubs

NIGHT ZONES

Vigorous nightlife takes place all over the city. Plaça Reial in the old town is always active, and the waterfront has really come alive with the opening of the Maremagnum shopping, restaurant, and entertainment complex, and the development of the Port Olímpic, where the action continues till dawn and beyond. There is a concentration of designer bars in the Eixample and Gràcia, with some of the smoother venues on the exclusive slopes of the wealthy suburb of Tibidabo.

ANTILLA BARCELONA

Come here and join Barcelona's Cuban residents for the best of real salsa and merengue in a wonderfully tacky setting—guaranteed good times and free dance lessons to get you going.

✚ F7 ✉ C/Aragó 141–143 ☎ 93 451 21 51 ⏰ Open daily at 11PM 🚇 Hospital Clinic

BIKINI

This large club in the basement of the L'Illa shopping mall has separate spaces for cocktails, salsa, and rock.

✚ F5 ✉ Déu I Mata 105 ☎ 93 322 00 05 ⏰ Closed Sun, Mon 🚇 Les Corts

LA BOÎTE

An eclectic mix of soul, funk, hip-hop, and Motown classics are on the turntable. Occasional live music.

✚ G6 ✉ Diagonal 477 ☎ 93 419 59 50 🚇 Diagonal

EL CAFÉ QUE PONE MUEBLES NAVARRO

Relax in squishy sofas and comfortable armchairs in this spacious lounge bar, which offers great cocktails and imaginative sandwiches.

✚ G8 ✉ C/Riera Alta 4–6 ☎ 607 18 80 96 ⏰ Closed Mon 🚇 San Antoni

CAFÉ ROYALE

Smouldering soul and flirty funk played to a crowd of models and hangers-on, at one of the hippest nightspots in the city.

✚ G9 ✉ C/Nou de Zurbano 3 ☎ 93 412 14 33 ⏰ Sun–Thu 6PM–2.30AM, Fri and Sat 6PM–3AM 🚇 Drassanes

CITY HALL

Three different levels blast out music spanning techno to deep-house, while lounging night owls chill-out on the terrace. One of downtown Barca's best for dancing the night away.

✚ H8 ✉ Rambla de Catalunya 2–4 ☎ 93 238 07 22 ⏰ Thu–Sat 1AM–6AM, Sun 1.30–6AM 🚇 Catalunya

C.D.L.C.

The new darling of FC Barcelona as this gig is owned by Patrick Kluivert's wife. It has Bedouin style "boudoirs" skirting the edge of the dance floor, two bars, and a restaurant, right at the water's edge.

✚ J10 ✉ Passeig Marítim 32 ☎ 93 224 04 70 ⏰ Daily noon–3AM 🚇 Ciutadella-Vila Olimpica

DANZATORIA

Barcelona's most beautiful night spot is the favoured haunt of visiting celebs. With sweeping staircases, sleek cocktail bars, designer lounges, steamy dance floors and breezy terraces, there is more than enough to keep even the most discerning night owls amused.

✚ H2 ✉ Av. Tibidabo 61 ☎ 93 206 49 50 ⏰ Daily 9–2.30AM, Fri and Sat 9–3AM 🚇 Av. Tibidabo

DOT LIGHT CLUB

Small, trendy night club behind the Plaça Reial with an intimate bar area and a dance floor where a top sound system delivers everything from chill-out electronic to house.

🏠 G9 ✉ C/Nou de Sant Fransesc 7 ☎ 93 302 70 26 🕙 Open daily from 10PM 🚇 Drassanes

DRY MARTINI

This elegant, ocean-liner style cocktail bar serves the best martinis in town to a mixed crowd of theatre goers, business men, party girls, and out-of-towners.

🏠 G6 ✉ C/Aribau 162–166 ☎ 93 217 50 72 🕙 Mon-Fri 1PM–2.30AM, Sat 6.30PM–3AM, Sun 6.30PM–2.30AM 🚇 Provença, Hospital Clínic, Diagonal

KARMA

This basement venue is still the most popular of several lively rock clubs around Plaça Reial.

🏠 G9 ✉ Plaça Reial 10 ☎ 93 302 56 80 🚇 Liceu

KGB

This stark shed of a building styled on a secret police theme attracts the hardiest of clubbing night owls; the action really begins only when dawn is approaching.

🏠 J5 ✉ Alegre de Dalt 55 ☎ 93 210 59 06 🚇 Joanic, Alfons X

LONDON BAR

Here since 1910, this former bohemian favourite, later taken up by local hippies, now draws an interesting, cosmopolitan mix of locals and young foreign residents. There's a stage at one end of the cavernous gallery, and occasional live music.

🏠 G9 ✉ Nou de la Rambla 34 ☎ 93 318 52 61 🚇 Paral.lel, Liceu

MOOG

Techno goes full blast at one of the city's trendiest clubs. Look for guest DJs from the international circuit. Chill-out room.

🏠 G9 ✉ Arc del Teatre 3 ☎ 93 301 72 82 🕙 Daily 🚇 Drassanes

OTTO ZUTZ

This club in a three-floor warehouse is still the place to see and be seen for Barcelona's glitterati and those aspiring to join them. Clever lighting and metal staircases and galleries set the scene.

🏠 H5 ✉ Lincoln 15 ☎ 93 238 07 22 🕙 Tue–Sat 🚇 Gràcia

LA TERRRAZZA

This huge, open-air, "Ibiza-style" club, behind the Poble Espanyol, functions during the summer as a place to dance the night away to some of the city's best dance music.

🏠 D/E8 ✉ Avda Marqués de Comillas ☎ 93 423 12 85 🕙 May–Oct: Thu–Sun from midnight 🚇 Espanya

TORRES DE AVILA

Design wizards Alfred Arribas and Javier Mariscal conjured up this series of symbol-loaded spaces in the twin towers guarding the entrance to the Poble Espanyol. Trance-techno discos are staged here at weekends. In summer there is a stunning view over the city from the rooftop terrace, with refreshing sea breezes.

🏠 D8 ✉ Marqués de Comillas, Poble Espanyol ☎ 93 424 93 09 🚇 Espanya 🚌 13, 61

DESIGNER METROPOLIS

Evidence of Barcelona's position at the sharp end of contemporary design can be seen all over the city, in squares, parks, street furniture, shopfronts, and interiors—even in the way gifts are packaged. In the 1980s, these talents were turned to the design of nightspots, each of which sought to upstage the rest.

Films, Theatre & Music

PAU CASALS

The great cellist, better known to the world as Pablo Casals (1876–1973), was a Catalan. In 1920, he helped push Barcelona onto Europe's musical map by founding his Barcelona Orchestra, which performed regularly in the Palau de la Música. In 1924–25, Igor Stravinsky directed the orchestra in concerts featuring his own works.

CINEMAS

Film-going is very popular in Spain, and queues are constant outside theatres before shows begin. Most first-run films are dubbed into Spanish or Catalan, but somewhere in town you can probably find a showing in the original version, especially in Gràcia's Verdi and Verdi Park theatres and in the Icària Yelmo complex at the Port Olímpic. Look in the ads for the notation VO (*versión original*).

FILMOTECA DE LA GENERALITAT DE CATALUNYA

The equivalent of a national cinema, with themed schedules of new and classic films, often in the original version.
❖ F5 ✉ Cinema Aquitània, Avinguda de Sarrià 31–33 ☎ 93 410 75 90 ⊕ Closed hols and Aug Ⓜ Hospital Clínic

COMPANIES AND ENSEMBLES

AUDITORI

This impressive venue is home for l'Orquestra, Simfònica de Barcelona i National de Catalunya.
❖ K8 ✉ Lepant 150 ☎ 93 247 93 00 Ⓜ Glòries

ELS COMEDIANTS

When not entertaining audiences abroad, the Comedians amaze fellow *Barcelonans* with an astonishing array of entertainment, including music, mime, dance, and tricks, often in the open air.

CENTRE CULTURAL DE LA CAIXA

The savings bank and Barcelona institution known as La Caixa has a vigorous cultural playlist that includes chamber concerts in one of its prestigious properties, the Casa Macaya, a *modernista* masterpiece by architect Puig I Cadafalch.
❖ J7 ✉ Passeig de Sant Joan 108 ☎ 93 458 89 07 Ⓜ Verdaguer

LA CUBANA

The original and best of the many groups mixing theatre, music, dance, and mime, La Cubana was founded in 1980 by Jordi Milan as a street theatre group. The original show, which ran for four years and was seen by over one million people, propelled the group to the heady heights of their own television show. They tour and perform at various venues and are now preparing a new act, incorporating films and improvisation.

LA FURA DELS BAUS

The highly talented Vermin of the Sewer perform at several venues around the city, with shows intended to maintain the shock of their name.

GRAN TEATRE DEL LICEU

Destroyed by fire in 1861, swiftly rebuilt, then burned again in 1994, the Lyceum holds a special place in the hearts of musical *Barcelonins*, since it was here that the city's passion for opera found its

prime expression.
The rebuilt Liceu
occupies an entire block
on the Lower Rambla and
the opera is back!

➕ G9 ✉ Rambla 61–65
☎ 93 485 99 00 Ⓜ Liceu

ELS JOGLARS

The Minstrels turn the
Catalan talent in dance
and mime to good account
in often startling satires.

MERCAT DE LES FLORS

The splendid halls of the
old flower market at the
foot of Montjüic now
serve as the main venue
for the annual Grec
Festival (➤ 4). During the
rest of the year, there is a
rich variety of dramatic,
dance, and concert events.

➕ E8 ✉ Lleida 59 ☎ 93
426 18 75 Ⓜ Espanya

ORFEÓ

A primary focus of the
Catalan revival around
the 1900s (the Palau de la
Música was built for
them), the Orfeó choir
still plays an important
role in the city's cultural
life, with its repertoire of
great classical works.

ORQUESTRA SIMFÒNICA DE BARCELONA I NACIONAL DE CATALUNYA

Now often known simply
as "L'Orquestra," this
orchestra is an object of
pride in Barcelona and
Catalonia as a whole, and
receives financial support
from both city and region.
In addition to playing
standard classical
repertoire, the orchestra is
also committed to
showcasing little-known
Catalan contributions to
serious music.

PALAU DE LA MÚSICA CATALANA (➤ 40)

One of the city's
unmissable architectural
sights, Domènech i
Montaner's Palace of
Music has long been
Barcelona's principal
auditorium, a splendid
setting for performances
by the Orfeó choir, the
Orquestra Simfònica, and
others. Reserve early.

➕ H8 ✉ Sant Francesc de
Paula 2 ☎ 93 295 72 00
Ⓜ Urquinaona

TEATRE LLIURE

The Free Theatre, housed
in a fine old Gràcia
building, is the home of
the well-established but
progressive company of the
same name, which has
built its reputation on
productions—in
Catalan—of classical and
contemporary drama. The
theatre also hosts dance
and poetry events and
concerts of 20th-century
music, and has a friendly
café-restaurant.

➕ H5 ✉ Montseny 47 ☎ 93
218 92 51 Ⓜ Fontana

TEATRE NACIONAL DE CATALUNYA

Built in the
undistinguished Plaça de
les Glòries Catalanes,
Ricardo Bofill's massive
new temple of theatre is
a postmodern homage to
classical Greek prototypes.

➕ K8 ✉ Plaça de les Arts 1
☎ 93 306 57 00
Ⓖ Guided tours on request
Ⓜ Glòries

BARCELONA–BAYREUTH

A century ago, a surge of
Wagnermania swept
Barcelona and his operas
remain popular today. The
composer's romanticism and
his ability to evoke a mythical
German past struck a chord
with Catalans engaged in
reviving their neglected and
suppressed nationhood; it was
all too easy to identify the
dragon as the common foe of
Siegfried and St. George,
Catalonia's patron saint.

Popular Music

JAZZ ROOTS

Barcelona's love affair with jazz goes back to the days before the Civil War, when Jack Hylton's dance band played at the International Exhibition and Django Reinhardt and Stéphane Grappelli brought the music of the Hot Club de France to the Hot Club de Barcelona. The tradition has been kept alive by such figures as the brilliant pianist Tete Monoliú and newcomer saxophonist Billy McHenry, and by the city's October Jazz Festival.

ANTILLA COSMOPOLITA

Buzzing and live Latin-American fare. The city's most popular venue of this type.
✚ G6 ✉ Aragón 141 ☎ 93 451 45 64 Ⓜ Hospital Clinic

BLUES CAFÉ

Live blues a couple of times a week, performed by local acts in an intimate Gràcia setting. Serves draft Guinness and Budvar.
✚ H5 ✉ La Perla 37 ☎ 93 416 09 65 Ⓜ Fontana

CLUB APOLO

Salsa and similar sounds fill this club in a former music hall.
✚ F/G9 ✉ Nou de la Rambla 113 ☎ 93 441 40 01 Ⓜ Paral.lel

LA COVA DEL DRAC

Barcelona's most venerable jazz establishment has a reputation for first-rate live music.
✚ G4 ✉ Vallmajor 33 ☎ 93 319 17 89 Ⓜ FGC Muntaner

HARLEM JAZZ CLUB

Intimate and popular Barri Gòtic club that's big with local and international jazz musicians.
✚ H9 ✉ Comtessa de Sobradiel 8 ☎ 93 310 07 55 🕐 Closed 2 weeks Aug Ⓜ Jaume I

JAMBOREE

An underground jazz club that's almost cave-like, hosting blues, soul, jazz, funk, and occasional hip-hop live bands. At 1AM on weekends, the dance floor opens and gets very crowded quite quickly.

Upstairs is Los Tarantos, a bar with predominantly Spanish music.
✚ G9 ✉ Plaça Reial 17 ☎ 93 301 75 64 Ⓜ Liceu

LUZ DE GAS

Another fine old converted music hall that's now an attractive venue for varied musical events. Jazz and salsa predominate.
✚ G6 ✉ Muntaner 246 ☎ 93 486 44 22 Ⓜ Diagonal

PALAU SANT JORDI

This masterpiece of modern architecture—a stadium in the Olympic Games turned music barn —hosts many of the big name bands that come to Barcelona.
✚ D9 ✉ Passeig Olympic s/n ☎ 93 426 20 89 Ⓜ Espanya

THE QUIET MAN

One of the city's best Irish bars has live Celtic music Thursday to Saturday.
✚ G9 ✉ Marqués de Berbera 11 ☎ 93 412 12 19 Ⓜ Liceu

RAZZMATAZZ

Three night-clubs and top-notch live music venue (especially for indie and electronica) in one, Razzmatazz has a loyal following.
✚ K8 ✉ C/Pamplona 88 ☎ 93 272 09 10 Ⓜ Marina

SONIQUETE

Small and smoky, this is the city's best bar for flamenco (both impromptu and planned) and an authentic *gitano* (gypsy) atmosphere.
✚ H9 ✉ C/Milans 5 ☎ 639 382 354, no English spoken Ⓜ Jaume I

Traditional Entertainment

DANCE VENUES

CENTRE ARTESI TRADICIONÀRIUS

Founded in 1993 for the study of traditional Catalan music, dance, and instruments, this comfortable, intimate theatre presents frequent performances.

➕ H5 ✉ Travessera de Sant Antoni 6–8 ☎ 93 218 44 85 Ⓜ Fontana

L'ESPAI

On the edge of village-like Gràcia, the Space (full name: L'Espai de Dansa i Música de la Generalitat de Catalunya) is the regional government-subsidized venue for performances of traditional and modern dance.

➕ G5 ✉ Travessera de Gràcia 63 ☎ 93 201 29 06 Ⓜ Diagonal

EL PATIO ANDALUZ

Not native to Catalonia, flamenco was brought here by immigrants from southern Spain after the Civil War. It has now put down roots, so you can enjoy great performances at a number of places, of which this is one.

➕ G6 ✉ Aribau 242 ☎ 93 209 33 78 🚌 58, 64

SALA BECKETT

This small, subterranean Gràcia theatre serves as a performance space for many of the better dance companies.

➕ J5 ✉ Alegre de Dalt 55 bis ☎ 93 284 53 12 Ⓜ Joanic

LOS TARANTOS

Here you will find some of the best flamenco acts in Catalonia. Conveniently located in Plaça Reial. You can dine while watching.

➕ G9 ✉ Plaça Reial 17 ☎ 93 318 59 66 Ⓜ Liceu

TABLAO DE CARMEN

This full-blooded flamenco show in touristy Poble Espanyol is none the worse for the setting—locals come here too. You can dine while watching the show, which is staged twice nightly.

➕ E8 ✉ Poble Espanyol ☎ 93 325 68 95 Ⓜ Espanya 🚌 13, 61

DANCE HALL

LA PALOMA

Robustly old-fashioned dance hall from the turn of the 20th century, with music to suit its wonderful mix of patrons from grandparents to grunge lovers.

➕ G8 ✉ Tigre 27 ☎ 93 301 68 97 Ⓜ Universitat

BULLRING

PLAÇA DE TOROS MONUMENTAL

Though it does have some following among native Catalans, bullfighting in Barcelona attracts mostly foreign tourists and visiting Spaniards. One of the city's big bull rings has now shut down; this one stages the *corrida* on spring and summer Sundays. It also has a museum, open during the bullfighting season (Apr–Sep).

➕ K7 ✉ Gran Via de les Corts Catalanes 749 ☎ 93 245 58 04 Ⓜ Monumental

OLD-FASHIONED FUN

El Molino, the most famous of Barcelona's music halls, may have closed down, but old-time cabaret and drag acts can still be found at a few spots. The Bodega Bohèmia (Lancaster 2) is the haunt of cabaret artistes who refuse to retire, while the ageing drag queens of El Cangrejo (The Crab), at Corsega 36, have become an imperishable city institution.

Luxury Hotels

PRICES

Expect to pay the following prices per night for a double room, but it's always worth asking when you make your reservation whether any special deals are available.

Budget	up to €90
Mid-range	up to €150
Luxury	over €150

RESERVING ACCOMMODATION

Barcelona is a great magnet for business visitors, and reserving early is a must if you are to have much choice in where to stay. The Olympic building boom boosted the number of luxury hotels, but also swept away some of the more modest accommodation. The concentration of hotels around the Rambla and within easy walking distance of Plaça de Catalunya makes this area of the city an obvious choice for first-time visitors.

ARTS BARCELONA

482 up-to-the-minute luxury rooms in two 44-floor towers, Spain's tallest buildings, over-looking the Port Olímpic.
🏠 J9 ✉ Marina 19–21 ☎ 93 221 10 00; fax 93 221 10 70 🚇 Ciutadella/Vila Olímpica

CLARIS

This late 19th-century town house, now a hotel of the greatest refinement, has restaurants, a fitness centre, Japanese garden, rooftop terrace with pool, and a museum of Egyptian antiquities. 124 rooms.
🏠 H7 ✉ Pau Claris 150 ☎ 93 487 62 62; fax 93 215 79 70 🚇 Passeig de Gràcia

COLÓN

An enviable location opposite the cathedral makes the Colón a favourite. From the 147 rooms, specify one up front, with a view of the cathedral, although the bells are very noisy.
🏠 H8 ✉ Avinguda del Catedral 7 ☎ 93 301 14 04; fax 93 317 29 15 🚇 Jaume I

CONDES DE BARCELONA

Close to the boutiques and shops on the Passeig de Gràcia, this superb building has nearly 200 ultra-comfortable rooms furnished in *modernista* style.
🏠 H7 ✉ Passeig de Gràcia 73–75 ☎ 93 467 47 80, fax 93 467 47 85 🚇 Passeig de Gràcia, Diagonal

GRAN HOTEL CATALONIA

Discreet decor and a central position make the Catalonia's 84 rooms an excellent choice at the lower end of this category.
🏠 G6 ✉ Balmes 142 ☎ 93 415 90 90; fax 93 415 22 09 🚇 Provença

GRAN HOTEL LA FLORIDA

Perched atop the Collserolla (Barcelona's mountainous back-bone) La Florida oozes class, from its individually designed romantic suites, down to glasses of water infused with rose petals.
🏠 off map ✉ C/de Vallvidrera al Tibidabo 83–93 ☎ 92 259 30 00, fax 93 259 30 01 🚇 None close by

GRAN HOTEL HAVANA

An exceptional example of *modernista* architecture in the Eixample, the 145-room Havana is bold but tastefully decorated.
🏠 H7 ✉ Gran Via de les Corts Catalanes 647 ☎ 93 412 11 15; fax 93 412 26 11 🚇 Passeig de Gràcia, Urquinaona

HOTEL OMM

This fashionable hotel is an eclectic mix of movie-set inspired interiors; Space Odyssey 2001 and the Matrix, meets down-home comfort and Feng Shui chic.
🏠 G6 ✉ C/Rosselló 265 ☎ 93 445 40 00; fax 93 445 4004 🚇 Diagonal

RIVOLI RAMBLAS

This 87-room hotel dating from the 1930s has beautiful art deco style and a terrace with a panorama over the Old City.
🏠 G8 ✉ Rambla 128 ☎ 93 302 66 43; fax 93 317 50 53 🚇 Catalunya

Mid-Range Hotels

BANYS ORIENTALS

Situated on one of the Born's most bustling streets, this friendly little hostal lives up to the area's style credentials without skimping on the service. A gem.

H9 ✉ C/Argenteria 37 ☎ 93 268 84 60, fax 93 268 84 61 🚇 Jaume 1

HOTEL CONSTANZA

Great value for money, this elegant, Japanese inspired boutique hotel is brilliantly situated for shopping and sights, plus it goes overboard on luxury complimentary toiletries.

H8 ✉ C/Bruc 33 ☎ 93 317 40 24 🚇 Urquinaona

DUQUES DE BERGARA

A prestigious edifice in *modernista* style in a fine location just off Plaça de Catalunya, offering great convenience and comfort in its 151 rooms.

G8 ✉ Bergara 11 ☎ 93 301 51 51; fax 93 317 34 42 🚇 Catalunya

GAUDÍ

No idle use of the great architect's name, this 73-room, modern hotel has an enviable location opposite the Palau Güell.

G9 ✉ Nou de la Rambla 12 ☎ 93 317 90 32; fax 93 412 26 36 🚇 Liceu

ORIENTE

At the somewhat seedy lower end of the Rambla, the mid-19th-century Oriente has long since ceased to be *the* place to stay in Barcelona, but its ornate public spaces and only slightly less alluring 142 bedrooms continue to attract customers who like lodgings with some character. Previous guests include Hans Christian Andersen and Errol Flynn.

G9 ✉ La Rambla 45 ☎ 93 302 25 58; fax 93 412 38 19 🚇 Liceu, Drassanes

HOTEL PRINCIPAL

This quiet hotel, just off the Ramblas has 60 good-sized rooms with modern bathrooms and a fuller range of services than most hotels in this category. The friendly, and professional service is an added bonus.

G9 ✉ C/Junta de Comerç 8 ☎ 93 318 89 70; fax 93 412 08 19 🚇 Liceu

HOTEL SANT ANGELO

A smallish hotel right beside the Joan Miró park, with good facilities, 48 comfortable rooms, and a relaxed lounge area which opens onto an inner courtyard.

F7 ✉ C/Consell de Cent 74 ☎ 93 423 46 47; fax 93 423 88 40 🚇 Rocafort/Tarragona

SUIZO

The welcoming Suizo is a good choice in the Barri Gòtic, with its 59 comfortable rooms.

H9 ✉ Plaça de l'Angel 12 ☎ 93 310 61 08; fax 93 315 04 61 🚇 Jaume I

HOTEL VIA AUGUSTA

This well-equipped hotel has 56 modern, airy rooms and good facilities. Transport links into the centre are excellent.

H5 ✉ Via Augusta 63 ☎ 93 217 92 50; fax 93 237 77 14 🚇 Fontana

SLEEPLESS CITY

Beware of noise. Barcelona is not a quiet city, and many of its citizens never seem to go to bed. A room on the Rambla may have a wonderful view, but without super-efficient double-glazing, undisturbed slumber cannot be guaranteed. Accommodation overlooking an unglamorous neighbouring skylight may be less picturesque but could prove a wiser choice.

Budget Accommodation

CAMPING

With the planned expansion of the airport, several of the campsites most convenient to the city centre are closing. It's worth heading north up the coast (the other side from the airport) to Masnou
✉ Carretera N2 км633, El Masnou ☎ 93 555 15 03
🕙 Open all year

ESPAÑA

The glory days of the España may be over, but the interiors of this turn-of-the-20th-century *modernista* edifice just off the Rambla—decorated by some of the finest artists of the time—still stand out. 80 rooms.
✚ G9 ✉ Sant Pau 9 ☎ 93 318 17 58; fax 93 317 11 34
🔵 Liceu

HOSTAL GAT RAVAL

This second-floor hostal provides everything the modern urban traveller needs, from internet access to abstract art impressions on the walls. Bathrooms are communal.
✚ G8 ✉ C/Joaquín Costa 44, 2 ☎ 93 481 66 70, fax 93 342 66 97 🔵 Universitat

GÒTICO

A well-established and comfortable choice in the centre of the Barri Gòtic. Upper end of the range, with 80 rooms.
✚ H9 ✉ Jaume I 14 ☎ 93 315 22 11; fax 93 268 90 62
🔵 Jaume I

HOSTAL LAUSANNE

Take the lift to reach this 17 room, 1st-floor *hostal* run by a friendly family. The spacious, high-ceilinged rooms are bright, and some have balconies.
✚ H8 ✉ Avda Portal de l'Angel 24 ☎ 93 302 11 39
🔵 Catalunya

HOSTAL OLIVA

Barcelona's swankiest street is not so exclusive that it is impossible to stay on it without paying a fortune. Here are bargain rooms, some with just a washbasin, in a 16-room *hostal* on the top floor of an Eixample apartment block.
✚ H7 ✉ Passeig de Gràcia 32 ☎ 93 488 01 62, fax 93 487 04 94 🔵 Passeig de Gràcia

INTERNACIONAL

The front rooms of this mid-sized hotel (60 rooms) have a bird's-eye view of the Rambla with its brightly-coloured paving pattern by Joan Miró.
✚ G9 ✉ Rambla 78–80 ☎ 93 302 25 66; fax 93 317 61 90 🔵 Liceu

MARINA FOLCH

No-frills, no-fuss accommodation but pleasant enough, with spruce, airy bedrooms all with en suite bathrooms. Close to the beach.
✚ H10 ✉ C del Mar 16 ☎ 93 310 37 09; fax: 93 310 53 27 🔵 Barceloneta

PASEO DE GRÀCIA

A corner site at the upper end of the city's most prestigious avenue and fine views from the upper rooms, make this 33 room, simple hotel an excellent choice.
✚ H6 ✉ Passeig de Gràcia 102 ☎ 93 215 58 24; fax 93 215 37 24 🔵 Passeig de Gràcia

PELAYO

The 15 idiosyncratic upper-floor rooms, located through an entrance hall shared with other establishments, feel more like someone's slightly chaotic home. But the place is adequate, and it's near to Plaça de Catalunya.
✚ G8 ✉ Pelai 9 ☎ 93 302 37 27; fax 93 412 31 68
🔵 Catalunya, Universitat

BARCELONA
travel facts

ESSENTIAL FACTS

Customs regulations

- The limits for non-EU visitors are 200 cigarettes or 50 cigars, or 250g of tobacco; 1 litre of spirits (over 22 percent) or 2 litres of fortified wine, 2 litres of still wine; 50g of perfume. The guidelines for EU residents (for personal use) are 800 cigarettes, 200 cigars, 1kg tobacco; 10 litres of spirits (over 22 percent), 20 litres of aperitifs, 90 litres of wine, of which 60 can be sparkling, 110 litres of beer.
- Travellers under 17 are not entitled to the tobacco and alcohol allowances.

Electricity

- The standard current is 220/225 volts AC (sometimes 110/125 volts AC).
- Plugs are of round two-pin type. US visitors require an adaptor and a transformer.

Etiquette

- It's normal to wish people *bon dia*. Friends exchange kisses on both cheeks.
- Expect to find unabashed smokers in public places.
- Do not wear shorts, short skirts, or skimpy tops in churches.

Lone and women travellers

- Barcelona is a reasonably female-friendly city, certainly compared with southern Spain. Women are unlikely to be hassled.

Money

- Foreign currency and travellers' cheques can be changed at banks and bureaux de change. Rates and commission vary; use ATMs.
- Major credit cards are in wide use.

Opening hours

- Bank hours: Mon–Sat 8.30–2, closed Sat in summer, though there are many local variations.
- Shops: Mon–Sat 9 or 10–1.30, 4.30–7.30 (hours are variable). Larger shops and department stores may open all day. Some Sunday opening.
- Restaurants: generally lunch 2–4, dinner 9–midnight (restaurants in tourist areas often open earlier).
- Many museums shut for lunch, close early on Sunday, and are shut all day Monday.

Places of worship

- Anglican: St. George's Church ✉ Horaci 38 ☎ 93 417 88 67 ⊙ Service Sun 11AM
- Mass in English: Parròquia Maria Reina ✉ Carretera d'Esplugues 103 ☎ 93 203 41 15 ⊙ Mass Sun 10AM

Student travellers

- Barcelona has a large student population and numerous hostels and youth hotels.
- Many museums give reduced-price admission to students.
- Information about youth activities is available from: Área de Asuntos Sociales y Juventud ✉ Carrer Ferran 32 ☎ 93 402 78 00
- Viva Youth and Student Travel ✉ Carrer Rocafort 116–122 ☎ 93 483 83 81

Restrooms

- Public restrooms are rare, but *servicios* can usually be found in department stores or museums.

Tourist offices

- Centre d'Informació, Plaça de Catalunya is the main centre of the city's tourist board. It has a hotel reservation office, bureau de change, and bookshop ⊙ daily 9–9
- Other information centres are at

the Ajuntament, Plaça Sant Jaume; the Estació Sants; and the Palau de Congressos, avda Reina Maria Cristina s/n. The Generalitat de Catalunya has its own tourist offices in the Palau Robert, Passeig de Gràcia. There is a tourist information booth at the Sagrada Familia from Jun–Sep.

- Uniformed tourist officials known as "Red Jackets" patrol popular tourist areas in summer.
- Officines d'Informació Turística are at airport terminals A and B.
- Information about cultural events can be found at Centre d'Informació de la Virreina ✉ **Palau de la Virreina, Rambla 99.**
- The Barcelona Card (valid for 1, 2, or 3 days) gives unlimited access to public transport and discounts at over 100 museums, monuments, restaurants, and shops. It is available from tourist information offices.

GETTING AROUND

Although Barcelona is a walker's city *par excellence*, at some point you will need to use the first-rate bus and metro (subway) system, which is supplemented by a number of oddities like funiculars and the last remaining tram line, the Tramvia Blau. Buses, the metro, and the suburban railway, FGC, are fully integrated and tickets can be used on any of them for either one-system or combined journeys. Pick up a map of the network from a tourist information centre or one of the TMB offices; these are in the metro stations at Plaça de la Universitat, Barcelona-Sants, and Sagrada Familia.

- Information line ☎ 010

Tickets

One-way tickets are available but it makes sense to pay for multiple journeys using one of several types of *targeta* (travelcard):

- *Targeta* 10 (or T-10) valid for 10 trips by metro (and FGC) or bus.
- *Targeta* 30/50 valid for 50 trips within 30 days by metro (and FGC) or bus.
- You must cancel one unit of a *targeta* per journey undertaken by inserting it into the automatic machine at the entry to a station or aboard a bus. Changing from metro (or FGC) to bus or vice versa within 1hr 15 mins counts as one trip.
- Passes for unlimited bus and metro use are available for 1 day, 2 days, 3 days, and 5 days.

Metro

- The network covers most parts of the city and is being extended Ⓒ Mon–Thu 5AM–midnight; Fri–Sat 5AM–2AM; Sun 6AM–midnight.

Trains

- Many main-line trains run beneath the city centre stopping at the underground stations at Passeig de Gràcia and Plaça de Catalunya.
- Rail information: National ☎ 902 240 202; International ☎ 93 490 11 22

Buses

- Bus is the most convenient way of reaching some important sights.
- More information (including frequency of service) is given on the panels at bus stops.
- There is a night service, the *Nitbus*, with routes centred around Plaça de Catalunya.
- Useful tourist routes include numbers 22 (Plaça de Catalunya-Gràcia-Tramvia Blau-Pedralbes Monastery) and 24 (Plaça de Catalunya-Gràcia-Parc Güell).

Taxi

- Barcelona's fleet of black-and-yellow taxis numbers 11,000.
- Fares are not unduly expensive.
- There are several phone cab firms
  ☎ 93 303 30 33/93 300 11 00/93 357 77 55/93 433 10 20
- For more information about public transportation ➤ 6–7

MEDIA & COMMUNICATIONS

Telephones

- New public phones accept coins, phonecards, and credit cards.
- Phonecards are available from paper shops and newsstands.
- Calls are cheaper after 10PM on weekdays, after 2PM Saturday, and all day Sunday.
- National operator ☎ 1009
- International operator: Europe ☎ 1008; elsewhere ☎ 1005
- You must dial Barcelona's code (93), even within Barcelona.
- To phone the US from Spain, prefix the code and number with 001.
- To phone the UK from Spain, dial 00 44, then drop the first zero from the area code.
- To phone Spain from the US, prefix the area code and number with 011 34; from the UK, 00 34.

Post offices

- Main post office (Correu Central)
  ✉ Plaça Antoni López ☎ 902 1971 97
  🕐 Mon–Sat 8.30AM–9.30PM, Sun 9AM–2.30PM
  🚇 Barceloneta. Address *poste restante* correspondence to Lista de Correos, 08070, Barcelona.
- Other post offices are at Plaça Bonsuccès, Ronda Universitat 23, and Carrer València 231.
- Stamps are sold at paper shops.
- Mailboxes are yellow and red.

Newspapers

- International papers can be found on the newsstands on the Rambla and Passeig de Gràcia.
- Papers published in Barcelona include the top seller *La Vanguardia* (Spanish—conservative, with current events supplement), *Avui* (Catalan—nationalist) and *El País* (Spanish—leftish, with listings supplement).
- The English-language monthly *Barcelona Metropolitan*, launched in 1996, has some listings and is free of charge.
- The main current events periodical is the weekly *Guía del Ocio*.
- *ANUNTIS* is a free listings periodical.

Radio

- BBC World Service on 15485, 12095, 9410, and 6195 Short Wave.
- There are four national radio stations.

EMERGENCIES

Emergency phone numbers

- Guardia Urbana (City police) ☎ 092
- Policía Nacional (National police) ☎ 091
- Ambulance ☎ 061
- Fire ☎ 080
- Turisme-Atenció (tourist assistance) ☎ 93 301 90 60
- General ☎ 012

Consulates

- Australia ✉ Gran Via Carles III 98 ☎ 93 490 90 13
- Canada ✉ Travessera de les Corts 265 ☎ 93 412 72 36
- Ireland ✉ Gran Via Carles III 94 ☎ 93 491 50 21
- New Zealand ✉ Travessera de Gràcia 64 ☎ 93 209 03 99
- United Kingdom ✉ Diagonal 477 ☎ 93 366 62 00
- United States ✉ Passeig Reina Elisenda 23 ☎ 93 280 22 27

Lost and found
- Servei de Troballes ✉ Ajuntament, Carrer Ciutat 9 ☎ 010

Medical treatment
- City centre emergency department (*urgència*) ✉ Centre d'Urgències Perecamps, Avinguda de les Drassanes 13–15 ☎ 93 441 06 00 🚇 Drassanes
- Check with your consulate to find private foreign-language doctors.
- Pharmacies (*Farmàcies*) offer a wider range of treatments and medicines than in many countries.
- Pharmacy opening hours Mon–Sat 9–1.30, 4.30–8. Every neighbourhood has a pharmacy open 24 hours on a rotating basis.

Sensible precautions
- Any place frequented by tourists may attract pickpockets and handbag-snatchers. The lower end of the Rambla and the Raval area have a reputation for this, but it can happen anywhere.
- Carry valuables in a money-belt or pouch, not in a pocket.
- Wear bags across the front of your body, not over the shoulder. Keep wearing bags and cameras when seated and keep an eye on belongings in cafés and bars.
- Beware of teams of operators: one may engage you in conversation while another neatly removes your wallet.

LANGUAGE

- Catalan now enjoys equal status to Castillian Spanish in Barcelona and Catalonia, and must *not* be thought of as a dialect.
- Street signs and official communications are now mostly in Catalan, but virtually everyone understands Castillian Spanish.
- Most people in the tourist industry speak some English and French.

- Any effort to speak Spanish or (especially) Catalan will be welcomed.

English	*Spanish/Catalan*
good morning	buenos días/bon dia
good evening	buenas tardes/bona tarda
good night	buenas noches/bona nit
hello	hola/hola
goodbye	adiós/adéu
thank you	gracias/gràcies
excuse me	perdóne
you're welcome	de nada/de res
please	por favor/si us pla
yes, no	si, no/sí, no
open	abierto/obert
closed	cerrado/tancat
church	iglesia/església
palace	palacio/palau
museum	museo/museu
street	calle/carrer
restroom, toilet	aseos, servicios/lavabo
Monday	lunes/dilluns
Tuesday	martes/dimarts
Wednesday	miércoles/dimecres
Thursday	jueves/dijous
Friday	viernes/divendres
Saturday	sábado/dissabte
Sunday	domingo/diumenge
1, 2	un (uno/una), dos/un (una), dos
3, 4	tres, cuatro/tres, quatre
5, 6	cinco, seis/cinc, sis
7, 8	siete, ocho/set, vuit
9, 10	nueve, diez/nou, deu

Index